Words to Relax:
Relaxation Scripts for Personal Growth and Stress Relief

Words to Relax:
Relaxation Scripts for Personal Growth and Stress Relief

Candi Raudebaugh
BScOT, MScOT, OT(C)

Inner Health Studio
Red Deer - Alberta - Canada

Inner Health Studio
PO Box 30036, 6380 50 Avenue
Red Deer, Alberta
Canada
T4N 1H7
words-to-relax@innerhealthstudio.com

Words to Relax: Relaxation Scripts for Personal Growth and Stress Relief

Published by Inner Health Studio

www.innerhealthstudio.com

ISBN 1449989985

EAN-13 9781449989989

The scripts in this book are from Inner Health Studio. Scripts like these are featured each week as a free relaxation download on the *Relaxation by Inner Health Studio* Podcast.

Audio recordings of many of these scripts are available to download free or for purchase at **www.innerhealthstudio.com**.

The author welcomes correspondence from readers at:

Candi Raudebaugh
PO Box 30036, 6380 50 Avenue
Red Deer, Alberta
Canada
T4N 1H7
words-to-relax@innerhealthstudio.com

Acknowledgements

Many people contributed to this book by providing ideas, assistance, and encouragement. I am grateful to my family, friends, and colleagues for their support.

I would like to thank Cherie Braden for her editing help. Her skillful editing ensured readability and improved the overall grammar and style of this book.

I am also grateful to Cherie Braden for her contribution to the *Relaxation for Improving One's Chess Game* script. Her ideas were essential to writing a script that included chess-specific terms and concepts relevant to those who play competitive chess.

I want to thank Ellie Martin Cliffe for her help with editing. Her knowledge and assistance helped to improve wording and grammar, and to maintain a style that is less clinical and more familiar.

I appreciate the ideas, suggestions, and requests from listeners of my *Relaxation by Inner Health Studio* podcast. Your ideas have been the inspiration for many of the relaxation scripts in this book.

Contents

Guided Imagery Scripts 77

Anxiety Relief Scripts 127

Guided Meditation Scripts 161

Conclusion: End of a Relaxation Script 343

References 357

About the Author 358

Introduction

Relaxation is a valuable skill that can improve mental and physical health.

This book is for anyone who would like to relax, record relaxation audio, or guide others to relax. Both professionals and nonprofessionals can use these relaxation scripts. Anyone who is experiencing stress and wants to relax will benefit from this book.

Decreased muscle tension, reduced pain, improved pain tolerance, mental clarity, lower blood pressure, an enhanced immune system, and a feeling of calm are just some of the benefits of relaxation. Achieve better health through visualization, guided imagery, meditation, progressive muscle relaxation, and more.

Relaxation really can change your life.

What is Relaxation?

Relaxation is the act of relaxing the mind and body, and can also be defined as the state of being relaxed.

During a relaxation exercise (such as progressive muscle relaxation, visualization, meditation, or another technique), muscle tension decreases, blood pressure goes down, the mind becomes calm, and the harmful effects of prolonged stress are counteracted.[1]

This "relaxation response" is the opposite of the stress response.[2]

The stress response is also known as the fight-or-flight response. The sympathetic nervous system is activated when we are in fight-or-flight mode. Over time, this can have all kinds of negative effects (which are the symptoms of stress).[3] The body naturally returns to a state of equilibrium through the activation of the relaxation response.[4]

The relaxation response is associated with lowered activity of the sympathetic nervous system, characterized by physiological changes that are the opposite of the changes seen with the fight-or-flight response. The heart rate decreases by an average of three beats per minute and the respiration rate decreases.[5] A restful state is achieved.

Though this response occurs automatically, it is also possible to learn how to activate the relaxation response deliberately using relaxation techniques, such as autogenics, progressive muscle relaxation, and meditation. Most people are not skilled at relaxation at first, but with practice, everyone can learn to relax. The relaxation response occurs more quickly and easily with practice.

---

[1] Benson, H. (1975). *The Relaxation Response*, 96. New York: Avon Books.

[2] Ibid., 73.

[3] www.innerhealthstudio.com/symptoms-of-stress.html

[4] Benson, H. (1975). *The Relaxation Response*, 97. New York: Avon Books.

[5] Ibid., 5.

Regularly inducing the relaxation response is most effective in improving day to day living and results in increased control over the body's responses to stress.

In his 1975 book, *The Relaxation Response*, pioneering relaxation researcher Herbert Benson noted that during a meditation exercise, the person may not feel different or notice any changes, but physiological changes are occurring nonetheless.[6] This means that whether or not you notice any changes at the time, by practicing relaxation techniques, the physical and psychological benefits of the relaxation response occur, and you are further protected against the harmful effects of stress.[7]

---

[6] Benson, H. T*he Relaxation Response*, 164.

[7] Ibid., 168.

Relaxation Safety

Some relaxation techniques (such as taking a few deep breaths) can be used anytime, anywhere to quickly relax. Other techniques (visualization, progressive relaxation, sleep relaxation, etc.) must be used only when it is safe to do so.

Potentially unsafe situations are those that require full alertness and responsiveness. **Please do not use relaxation techniques or listen to audio recordings of relaxation scripts while in situations that require you to be alert (for example, while driving).**

None of the relaxation exercises should cause pain. If experiencing physical or emotional discomfort, stop, ease up, or take a break. Always listen to your body when using relaxation. If you are a facilitator who is helping others to relax, make sure to explain how to use relaxation safely.

People who have a history of trauma may find that some of the images or suggestions, or even the idea of trying to relax, can create anxiety. While it can be therapeutic to endure some discomfort at times, remember to take breaks or stop the relaxation exercise before becoming overwhelmed.

Only endure discomfort when you are ready and able to do so safely, and keep any discomfort within manageable limits. Relaxation techniques can be introduced gradually to get rid of anxiety that may initially accompany relaxation efforts.

Avoid using visualization, autogenics, or imagery techniques when experiencing severe psychosis or problems with reality orientation, as such techniques can worsen hallucinations.[8]

If you have concerns about using relaxation techniques, consult a professional who is knowledgeable about relaxation.

---

[8] Kathlyn L. Reed. (2001). *Quick Reference to Occupational Therapy, Second Edition*, 764. Aspen Publishers Inc. Gaithersburg, Maryland.

General Tips for Relaxing

1. Adopt a **passive attitude**. Approach relaxation with a "let it be" perspective.[9] Don't try to make anything happen. Even if you do not feel different, you still experience the benefits of relaxation. Be assured that the relaxation technique *is* working.

2. Relax in a **quiet environment** with few distractions. As you become more familiar with relaxation and have practiced various techniques, you will learn to relax anywhere. To begin, however, choose an environment that is free of distractions.

3. Make sure you are in a setting that does not require your outside attention. **Keep yourself safe.** Review the relaxation safety section on the preceding page for more details.

4. **Make yourself comfortable.** Position yourself on a chair with neck and back support, a firm bed, or a comfortable mat on the floor. Make sure the room is warm; not too hot or too cool. Choose a comfortable position that you can maintain for at least 10 minutes.

5. **Start with short relaxation sessions**; about 5 minutes. With more experience, achieving relaxation will become easier and you will be able to relax for longer periods of time. With practice, a duration of 20 or 30 minutes is quite reasonable, and you may wish to relax for even longer sessions.

6. **Your own voice** can be particularly effective for inducing the relaxation response, because people often respond best to suggestions they provide themselves. You might find you are able to relax listening to your own voice better than listening to the voice of someone else.

7. Relaxation is a skill that must be learned. **Practice often**—every day is best.

---

[9] Benson, H. (1975). *The Relaxation Response*, p 160. New York: Avon Books.

8. **Set aside time to relax each day**. Some people prefer to relax right
    before bed to help themselves fall asleep. Others relax first thing in
    the morning to start the day refreshed and revitalized. Consider
    whether there are times in the day when your stress level is high or
    your energy is low. These can be ideal times to schedule a brief
    relaxation session.

9. **Keep experimenting**. No one method of relaxation will work for
    everyone. It is important to try out different strategies to see which
    ones work best. There is no right or wrong way to relax.

Guidelines for Recording and Using Relaxation Audio

1. Read the script slowly in a calm voice. Pause frequently. It is very common to read too quickly—what seems to be a very slow pace when reading, is not nearly as slow when listening. Take two or three breaths between each phrase. Pausing in the middle of a phrase can be effective, too.

2. Concentrate on saying each word clearly and slowly—but not so slow as to cause distraction, and without elongating the words (a bit of practice will help you adjust your reading style to your own preferences).

3. For optimal voice clarity, remain well hydrated and wait at least half an hour after eating to read relaxation scripts. Some foods can affect the mucus of the throat and result in a less clear voice for several minutes after eating.

4. A high-quality microphone can make a significant difference in the quality of audio recordings. A computer's internal microphone is usually not good enough to make clear recordings. A microphone that connects to a computer through a USB port can be obtained relatively inexpensively, and enables digital audio recording and editing.

5. A tape recorder is a good option for the lowest-cost audio recordings, if advanced editing is not needed.

6. Listen to audio recordings of relaxation scripts at a low volume, adjusted to be loud enough to hear without straining, but quiet enough to be calm and relaxing.

7. Background music can help create a calming atmosphere. Choose relaxing music without lyrics, and play at a low volume to allow the spoken script to be heard clearly above the music.

Guidelines for Reading Scripts Out Loud for Others

1. Use a quiet location. Dim or turn off the lights, if possible.

2. Offer comfortable chairs and mats if available, so participants can sit or lie down, or have participants sit in firm chairs or cross-legged on the floor.

3. Read in a clear voice that is just loud enough that participants can hear without straining, but still quiet enough to be calming. If the room or the group is too large for each participant to hear a normal speaking voice, use a microphone to amplify your voice.

4. Watch participants' breathing and movement to ensure that your instructions are well-timed. Wait for participants to complete actions (such as tensing and relaxing a muscle group) before continuing with further instructions.

5. Review any relevant safety information before beginning the relaxation exercise. For example, before doing physical relaxation techniques, tell participants to listen to their bodies and refrain from doing any movements that cause pain.

6. Give participants a minute or two at the end of the relaxation exercise to fully reawaken. Use a script conclusion that guides participants to return to full alertness.

Relaxation Challenges: Applying Relaxation to Everyday Life

Most people who try relaxation find that it is both helpful and enjoyable. Even so, most find it difficult to fit relaxation into daily life. Relaxation is vital to health and well-being, but unfortunately, taking care of oneself is often something that is put off for later. With daily hassles, pressures, and demands, the activities that promote a good quality of life can be some of the easiest things to postpone.

Neglecting self-care can be a costly mistake. Stress overload, burnout, and exhaustion can make it impossible to continue to fulfill the demands that had been taking priority. Relaxation can help overloaded individuals to recover from burnout. It can also prevent burnout from occurring, especially if relaxation is used regularly. Making relaxation a priority can contribute to optimal functioning and a better quality of life.

Ideally, relaxation needs to be practiced every day, even if for just a few minutes.

Tips for Fitting Relaxation into a Busy Schedule

Start Small
Do a one-minute relaxation technique, such as calm breathing or a short, five-minute relaxation exercise.

Short and Quick
Practice short, quick relaxation techniques throughout the day.

Make a New Habit
Make relaxation a new habit. Think about what sort of habit would fit well with your schedule and your preferences.

Some possibilities to consider:

- Listen to relaxation scripts just before bed. When you have nothing else to do besides sleep, it can be easier to be still for the duration of a relaxation exercise. Another benefit is that practicing relaxation just before bed can help you unwind and prepare for sleep.

- Take a class so you have a regularly scheduled relaxation activity (for example: yoga, painting, music lessons, or tai chi).

- Try doing a relaxation activity (progressive muscle relaxation or yoga, for instance) first thing in the morning to help calm and energize you.

- Consider other times of day that might work for you: lunchtime, coffee break, right after work, or whenever might best suit your preferences.

- Schedule relaxation and make this self-care routine a priority. Relaxation can be as regular as brushing your teeth or eating lunch.

Relaxation Journal

This Relaxation Journal will allow you to monitor your physical and emotional symptoms and evaluate the effectiveness of the relaxation techniques you try. Feel free to photocopy the Relaxation Journal for your own use or to use with others.*

Begin at the top of the block by indicating the present date, describing the stressful situation, and circling the rating for your current stress level. List the physical and emotional symptoms of stress you are experiencing. Then do a relaxation or coping technique.

After practicing the technique, write down what you did and rate your current stress level. Describe the result of the relaxation or coping activity.

You can then use this journal to determine which relaxation techniques are most effective for you, which times of day tend to be the most stressful, and which times of day relaxation works the best. You can also see your progress by noticing changes in your overall stress level.

*The Relaxation Journal can be copied as needed for personal use, or to use with others, provided that Inner Health Studio is credited by keeping page headers intact. The Relaxation Journal is not for resale. It can be used within paid client sessions, but only as a free resource and not for any fee above the cost of photocopying.

Relaxation Journal

Date:	Time:

Stressful Situation:

Stress level before using a relaxation or coping technique (0 - Completely relaxed; 10 - Total panic):

0   1   2   3   4   5   6   7   8   9   10

Symptoms of stress and anxiety (list the symptoms you are experiencing right now):

Now do a coping or relaxation technique.

Technique used:

Stress level after using a relaxation or coping technique (0 - Completely relaxed; 10 - Total panic):

0   1   2   3   4   5   6   7   8   9   10

Result:

Notes:

Example

Date: *January 1*	Time: *7:15 PM*

Stressful Situation:

I forgot that I had promised my friend we would meet for dinner, and when I got home there was a message on my machine.

Stress level before using a relaxation or coping technique (0 - Completely relaxed; 10 - Total panic):

0   1   2   3   4   5   6   7   8   (9)   10

Symptoms of stress and anxiety (list the symptoms you are experiencing right now):

Headache, cold hands, stomach upset, feel guilty.

Now do a coping or relaxation technique.

Technique used:

I phoned my friend to apologize and reschedule, then did progressive muscle relaxation.

Stress level after using a relaxation or coping technique (0 - Completely relaxed; 10 - Total panic):

0   1   (2)   3   4   5   6   7   8   9   10

Result:

I felt much better after resolving the situation and doing the relaxation technique.

Notes:

I think I will write our next dinner date on the calendar.

Fit Relaxation with Your Spiritual Beliefs

Relaxation can be a meaningful experience and a spiritual practice, but does not need to be associated with any particular religion or spiritual path. The scripts in this book are intended to be neutral without particular religious references, except for some examples of meditation phrases in the Spiritual Meditation Script. This neutrality allows you to customize the relaxation experience to your own spiritual beliefs.

Occupational therapists define spirituality as the core of a person; the source of meaning for an individual.[10] This may or may not include religion. Everyone has spirituality, and each individual's spirituality is unique.

Meditation that includes your beliefs or spirituality is even more effective than meditating upon something neutral.[11] These relaxation scripts can be combined with prayer, meaningful music, or other spiritual elements to tailor the relaxation experience to your personal preferences.

---

[10] www.innerhealthstudio.com/occupational-therapy.html

[11] Benson, H. (1975). *The Relaxation Response*. New York: Avon Books.

Relaxation Techniques

The scripts in this book are divided into categories according to the techniques used. Several of the scripts use multiple techniques, and most of the scripts could fit into more than one category, but for simplicity, each script is listed in just one of the following:

Visualization
Visualization is the process of achieving relaxation by picturing a relaxing setting.

Guided Imagery
Guided imagery can be used to visualize positive actions, changes, or accomplishments.

Relaxation for Anxiety Relief
Anxiety relief scripts are specifically targeted at reducing anxiety in the moment by calming the mind and body.

Guided Meditation
Meditation is the act of focusing the mind to relax, improve inner awareness, and make positive mental or physical changes.

Physical Relaxation Techniques
Physical relaxation involves a variety of physical relaxation exercises, whether by focusing on a specific muscle group, tensing and relaxing muscle groups, moving, or stretching.

Creative Expression Relaxation
Creative relaxation scripts allow you to relax using creative outlets: art, music, movement, or other forms of self-expression.

Quick Relaxation
These quick relaxation scripts provide strategies to relax quickly, at any time, in any place.

Sleep Relaxation
Sleep relaxation scripts are specifically aimed to help you quickly and easily fall asleep. They do not include a reawakening conclusion, but rather, end with drifting off to sleep.

Autogenics
"Autogenic" means self-generated. Autogenic relaxation involves imagining physical changes in the body that are associated with the relaxation response; for example, imagining that the limbs are warm and heavy, and breathing is slow and regular.

Sensory Relaxation
These sensory relaxation scripts involve the use of the senses (sight, sound, touch, taste, and smell) to bring about relaxation. This may involve imagining or experiencing different sensations.

Relaxation for Children
These relaxation scripts for children can be used to guide children or adults to relax using quick and easy relaxation techniques.

Please note that these relaxation scripts are intended to be used with the guidance of an adult. Ensure that a parent or guardian reviews the scripts and is available to supervise their use as needed. Relaxation is safe and effective for people of all ages, provided it is used wisely, and not when the subject needs to be awake and alert.

Personalized Relaxation Scripts
Create your own relaxation scripts using these elements. Choose any induction, body, and conclusion from the list that follows, or adapt existing relaxation scripts by replacing parts of the script with different induction or conclusion portions.

Relaxation Scripts

Visualization Scripts

Beach Visualization

Visualization relaxation is an effective way to relax the mind and body by picturing a relaxing scene. This script guides you to imagine relaxing on a beautiful beach.

Start reading the script here:

Get comfortable. Sit in a supportive chair or lie on your back.

Relax your body by releasing any areas of tension. Allow your arms to go limp...then your legs...

Feel your arms and legs becoming loose and relaxed...

Now relax your neck and back by relaxing your spine...release the hold of your muscles all the way from your head, down your neck...along each vertebra to the tip of your spine...

Breathe deeply into your diaphragm, drawing air fully into your lungs...and release the air with a whooshing sound...

Breathe in again, slowly...pause for a moment...and breathe out...

Draw a deep breath in...and out...

In...out...

Become more and more relaxed with each breath...

Feel your body giving up all the tension...becoming relaxed...and calm... peaceful...

Feel a wave of relaxation flow from the soles of your feet, to your ankles, lower legs, hips, pelvic area, abdomen, chest, back, hands, lower arms, elbows, upper arms, shoulders, neck, back of your head, face, and the top of your head...

Allow your entire body to rest heavily on the surface where you sit or lie. Now that your body is fully relaxed, allow the visualization to begin.

Imagine you are walking toward the ocean...walking through a beautiful, tropical forest...

You can hear the waves up ahead...you can smell the ocean spray...the air is moist and warm...feel a pleasant, cool breeze blowing through the trees...

You walk along a path...coming closer to the sea...as you come to the edge of the trees, you see the brilliant aqua color of the ocean ahead...

You walk out of the forest and onto a long stretch of white sand...the sand is very soft powder...imagine taking off your shoes, and walking through the hot, white sand toward the water...

The beach is wide and long...

Hear the waves crashing to the shore...

Smell the clean salt water and beach...

You gaze again toward the water...it is a bright blue-green...

See the waves washing up onto the sand...and receding back toward the ocean...washing up...and flowing back down...enjoy the ever-repeating rhythm of the waves...

Imagine yourself walking toward the water...over the fine, hot sand... you are feeling very hot...

As you approach the water, you can feel the mist from the ocean on your skin.

You walk closer to the waves, and feel the sand becoming wet and firm...

A wave washes over the sand toward you...and touches your toes before receding...

As you step forward, more waves wash over your feet...feel the cool water provide relief from the heat...

Walk further into the clear, clean water...you can see the white sand under the water...

The water is a pleasant, relaxing temperature...providing relief from the hot sun...cool but not cold...

You walk further into the water if you wish...swim if you want to... enjoy the ocean for a few minutes...allow the relaxation to deepen... more and more relaxed...enjoy the ocean...

(Pause)

Now you are feeling calm and refreshed...

You walk back out of the water and onto the beach...

Stroll along the beach at the water's edge...free of worries...no stress... calm...enjoying this holiday...

Up ahead is a comfortable lounge chair and towel, just for you...

Sit or lie down in the chair, or spread the towel on the sand...relax on the chair or towel...enjoying the sun...the breeze...the waves...

You feel peaceful and relaxed...allow all your stresses to melt away...

(Pause)

When you are ready to return from your vacation, do so slowly...

Bring yourself back to your usual level of alertness and awareness...

Keep with you the feeling of calm and relaxation...feeling ready to return to your day...

Open your eyes, stretch your muscles...and become fully alert... refreshed...and filled with energy.

Forest Visualization

This Forest Visualization is a guided visualization script in which you imagine walking through a beautiful forest in the mountains.

Start reading the script here:

Begin by finding a comfortable position sitting or lying down. Allow your body to begin to relax as you start to create a picture in your mind.

Imagine yourself walking on a path through a forest. The path is soft beneath your shoes, a mixture of soil, fallen leaves, pine needles, and moss. As you walk, your body relaxes and your mind clears, more and more with each step you take.

Breathe in the fresh mountain air, filling your lungs completely...now exhale...breathe out all the air. Feeling refreshed.

Take another deep breath in...revitalizing...and breathe out completely, letting your body relax further.

Continue to breathe slowly and deeply as you walk through the forest and continue the forest visualization.

The air is cool, but comfortable. Sun filters through the trees, making a moving dappled pattern on the ground before you.

Listen to the sounds of the forest...birds singing...a gentle breeze blowing. The leaves on the trees shift and sway in the soft wind.

Your body relaxes more and more as you walk. Count your steps and breathe in unison with your strides.

Breathe in...2...3...4...hold...2...3...exhale...2...3...4...5...

Breathe in...2...3...4...hold...2...3...exhale...2...3...4...5...

Breathe in...2...3...4...hold...2...3...exhale...2...3...4...5...

Continue to breathe like this, slowly and deeply, as you become more and more relaxed.

As you walk through the forest, feel your muscles relaxing and lengthening. As your arms swing in rhythm with your walking, they become loose, relaxed, and limp.

Feel your back relaxing as your spine lengthens and the muscles relax. Feel the tension leaving your body as you admire the scenery around you.

Your legs and lower body relax as well, feeling free and relaxed.

As you continue to walk through the forest, you begin to climb a slight incline. You easily tread along smooth rocks on the path. Feeling at one with nature.

The breeze continues to blow through the treetops, but you are sheltered on the path, and the air around you is calm.

Small saplings grow at the sides of the path.

Around you is an immense array of greens. Some of the leaves on the trees are a delicate, light green. Some leaves are deep, dark, true forest green.

Many trees have needles that look very soft and very green. The forest floor is thick, green moss.

Tall trees grow on either side of the path. Picture the variety of trees around you. Some have smooth, white bark. Others are darker, with coarse, heavy bark, deeply grooved. Enjoy the colors of the bark on the trees—white, tan, brown, red, black...many combinations of color. You admire the rough, brown bark of pine trees and enjoy the fresh pine scent.

Smell the forest around you. The air is fresh, and filled with the scent of trees, soil, and mountain streams.

You can hear the sound of water faintly in the distance. The gentle burbling sound of a creek.

As you continue to walk through the forest, you are gaining elevation and getting closer to the sound of a running stream.

Continue to enjoy the forest around you.

As you near the top of the mountain, you hear the stream, very close now. The path curves up ahead. You can see sunlight streaming onto the path.

As you round the corner, you hear the water, and see a clearing in the trees up ahead. A beautiful look out point awaits.

You are growing tired from your journey. Your body feels pleasantly tired and heavy.

Imagine yourself walking toward the clearing and the stream. Stepping stones make an easy path across the stream and toward the edge of the mountain. Step on each large flat stone to easily cross the small, shallow stream.

Up ahead is a large, smooth rock...like a chair waiting for you to rest. The rock is placed perfectly, high up on this beautiful vantage point.

Sit or lie down on the rock if you wish. It is very comfortable. You feel very comfortable and at ease. The sun shines down on you.

Looking around, you see mountains in the distance. Faint and blue.

You can look down from your vantage point into a valley with trees and a brilliant blue lake. Across from you is another mountain.

The clearing around you is made up of rocks, soil, pine needles, moss, and grass. The grass and mountain wildflowers around you blow gently in the breeze. A deer quietly emerges from the edge of the forest to graze in the clearing. As the deer raises its head to look at you, you can see it's nostrils moving to catch your scent. The deer cautiously walks to the stream to drink before disappearing back into the forest.

Squirrels dart in and out of sight as they romp through the trees, and race across the clearing.

Feel the sun warming your body as you relax on the rock. Enjoy the majestic landscape around you and feel your body relaxing even more.

Your body becomes very warm, and very heavy.

Continue to breathe the clean, fresh air.

You feel so relaxed.

Calm.

At peace.

In unity with nature around you.

Enjoy the sights...sounds...and smells of the forest around you.

Feel the sun, warm on your skin.

Feel the gentle breeze blow across your cheek.

Listen to the birds singing.

Hear the stream flowing. The leaves rustling in the breeze. Squirrels chattering.

See the flowers, trees, valley, and mountains around you.

Lie back on the comfortable rock, and you can look up to see the blue sky. Small white clouds float gently across the sky. Watch them drift slowly by. Shapes ever changing.

Enjoy this peaceful place.

(Pause)

When you are ready to leave this peaceful place, slowly begin to reawaken your body.

Know that you can return to this forest visualization in your imagination whenever you like.

As you reawaken, keep with you the feeling of calm, peace, and relaxation.

Wiggle your fingers and toes to wake up your muscles.

Shrug your shoulders. Stretch if you want to.

When you are ready, open your eyes and return to full wakefulness, feeling alert and refreshed.

Candle Visualization Relaxation

This candle relaxation is a guided visualization script in which I'll help you to imagine relaxing while looking at a candle. You can relax your body and mind by focusing on the candle.

Start reading the script here:

To begin, find a comfortable position. Take note of how your body feels. Take a deep breath in, and as you exhale, notice where your body feels the most tense.

Focus on these areas as you take another breath.

Allow the tension to flow away as you breathe out.

Inhale as you raise your shoulders...then relax as you exhale, and lower your shoulders into a comfortable position.

Continue to breathe smoothly and gently.

As you rest peacefully, begin to form an image in your mind. Imagine that you are in a safe, comfortable room. The room is pleasantly dark.

Imagine the glow of a candle beside you. Keep your attention facing forward as you notice the gentle flickers of warm light on the wall in front of you. See the dancing light from the candle.

Feel yourself relaxing as you watch the beautiful patterns made by the light of the candle.

You might want to turn to look at the candle. If you wish, turn your imagination toward the candle.

Picture the candle in front of you, and see the soft light it creates.

Notice the flame gently moving as the candle burns.

Imagine what the candle looks like. What shape is it? What color? What size?

Create a picture of the candle in your mind.

Imagine that the candle gently melts away the stresses and tension you have been holding in your body. As the candle burns, feel the tension easing, and relaxation flowing through your body.

Notice the wax becoming softer. Feel your body also becoming softer.

Notice again the soft flame at the top of the candle. See how it flickers slightly in response to your breath as you exhale. Watch how the flame responds each time you breathe.

Now turn your attention back to the wax of the candle. The softening wax is melting, turning to liquid. Warm and flowing...free from tension...

See the wax of the candle melting...melting the way your tension is melting away.

As the melted wax builds, see it slowly overflow, and pour down the side of the candle, drop by drop.

It feels like any stresses you were holding on to are dripping away with each drop of wax from the candle. The soft flame of relaxation warms you from the inside, melting away all stress.

Watch the wax melting...feeling the same effects on the tension in your body. Melting...relaxing.

Continue to observe the burning candle, enjoying the relaxation you are experiencing.

When you are ready to finish your relaxation session, take a deep breath...and exhale through your mouth, blowing out the candle.

Slowly bring your awareness back to the present.

Become more aware of the time and place you are in today.

Slowly stretch your muscles...and open your eyes...enjoying the feeling of calm and peace that remains with you.

Calming Color Relaxation Visualization

This calming color relaxation script allows you to relax with visualization by imagining each color of the rainbow.

Begin reading the calming color relaxation script here:

To begin, make yourself comfortable. Adjust your clothing as needed and assume a comfortable position.

First, before the calming color relaxation begins, notice how your body feels in this moment.

Passively pay attention to the state of your body right now. Do not try to change anything, simply notice how your body and mind feel.

Feel your body begin to relax slightly, as your shoulders drop a little lower...your jaw loosens so your teeth are not touching...and your eyelids start to feel heavy.

Take a deep breath in...hold it...and slowly breathe out...

Now just notice your breathing. Your body knows how much air you need. Notice with interest how your breath goes in and out. Feel the pause after you inhale and before you exhale...and the pause before drawing another breath.

Allow your body to relax and your mind to focus on the calming colors.

Allow the relaxation to occur naturally...allow and observe...

Create a picture in your mind of the color red.

Imagine reds of all shades...

You might picture red objects, a red landscape, or just a solid color...

Imagine all the different tones of red...roses...bricks...apples...sunset...

Enjoy the color red.

(Pause)

Now allow the color you are imagining to change to orange.

Picture the color orange...infinite shades of orange...flowers...
pumpkins...carrots...

Fill the entire visual field of your mind's eye with the color orange.

Enjoy the color orange.

(Pause)

Visualize the color yellow. See in your imagination all the various shades
of yellow.

Allow yellow to fill your vision...lemons...flowers...fall leaves...

Imagine the endless tones of the color yellow. Imagine yourself
surrounded with the calming color yellow...immerse yourself...

Enjoy the color yellow.

(Pause)

Let the color you are imagining become green. Fill your imagination
with the color green.

Endless shades and tones of green...plants...leaves...grass...

Imagine being surrounded by beautiful green...all shades from the lightest to the darkest, bright green...subdued green...

(Pause)

Enjoy green.

Now see in your mind the color blue. Surround yourself with beautiful blue...

Unending shades of blue...water...sky...

Imagine blue filling your vision...

Enjoy the color blue.

(Pause)

Allow the color in your imagination to become violet.

Focus on the multitude of purples around you...flowers...eggplant...sunrise...

Immerse yourself in the color violet...

Enjoy violet.

(Pause)

Now allow your attention to return to your breathing...notice how calm and regular your breathing is now...

Meditate on the calming colors once more...imagine the colors again, one at a time...starting with red...

Orange...

Yellow...

Green...

Blue...

Violet...

Now picture whatever calming color you wish. Do you have a favorite? Or a color that suits your mood right now?

Imagine whatever colors you like. Allow your mind to be relaxed, focused, and calm...

Enjoy the feeling of relaxation you are experiencing...

(Pause)

Now it is time to return your attention to your regular activities.

Become more alert with each breath you take...

More aware of your surroundings...

Stretch your muscles...and open your eyes. Fully alert and calm.

Floating on a Cloud

This relaxation script is a calming visualization that will guide you to imagine floating on a cloud.

Begin reading the relaxation script here:

Find a relaxed position—lying down is best—and get comfortable.

First, relax your body. Starting at the top of your head, allow a feeling of relaxation to begin. Feel the relaxation grow with each breath you take.

Inhale...relax your scalp and head...exhale...let the tension go away even more...

Breathe in relaxation...feeling your face and ears relax...exhale all the tension.

Inhale...feeling your neck and shoulders relaxing...

As you exhale, let all the muscles of your neck and shoulders release their hold, relaxing fully...

Breathe in, feeling the relaxation continuing to your arms and hands... breathe out the tension...

Breathe in relaxation...allowing your chest and upper back to relax... release the tension as you exhale.

Inhale, feeling the relaxation flowing through your middle back and your stomach...release the muscles of your back and stomach as you breathe out...

As you take another breath, feel your lower back relaxing. Feel the tension leaving as you release the breath.

Breathe in, relaxing your hips and pelvic area...breathe out, relaxing even further.

As you inhale, feel your upper legs relaxing...let the muscles of your legs completely let go as you breathe out.

Take another breath drawing in relaxation, all the way down to your feet. Let your legs go limp as you exhale.

Continue to breathe in relaxation, and breathe out tension.

(Pause)

Now you are feeling deeply relaxed. Deeply relaxed and calm...

Begin to create a picture in your mind. Imagine that you are floating on a soft, fluffy white cloud.

Feel the surface beneath you becoming softer...more cloud-like...feel the cloud rising out of the surface you are on, surrounding you in it's protective support...soon you are floating on just the cloud...

Let it rise a little further, taking you with it...see the walls and ceiling around you disappearing as you float into the sunny sky...drifting on the cloud.

Feel the cloud beneath you. It is soft but supportive. Feel the cloud supporting your whole body.

Notice each place where your body is touching the cloud. Feel how soft and comfortable the cloud is. It is almost like floating in the air.

Notice how the cloud feels. It might be a little bit cool, and moist, like fog.

Your body is warm, very warm and heavy, and sinking into the cloud. It is a wonderful feeling.

Start to create an image in your mind of where you are. You might be floating just barely above the ground. You can choose to float wherever you like. The sky above you is bright blue, sunny, and inviting. You are warm and comfortable, warmed by the sun's rays shining down peacefully.

There are some other clouds in the sky, floating gently. See them lazily passing by, far above.

Your cloud can float wherever you choose. If you enjoy being high up, you can let your cloud rise into the sky. It is very safe. Very calming. Very relaxing. You are so relaxed. Floating on a cloud. Supported gently but firmly by your cloud.

Surrounded by the cloud's protective embrace.

See the sights around you. Imagine the green grass below, gently blowing in the wind. The grass recedes further away as you rise into the sky. From here, the grass looks like a soft carpet, the wind creating gentle waves in the grass as if it were water.

What else do you see? Perhaps some trees, their leaves whispering in the gentle breeze. You can gaze down on housetops, country roads, hills.

From this amazing vantage point, you can see around you 360 degrees. The horizon stretches out in a complete circle around you.

Notice in the distance how the hills appear almost blue...slightly hazy.

How does it feel to be floating on a cloud? Does it sway gently, like a boat on almost-smooth water? Does it drift in the breeze? Can you feel the movement as you gently float on the cloud? You feel so comfortable...so relaxed...

Floating on a cloud...

(Pause)

Continue floating on the cloud, enjoying the sights around you. Up here, the air is so clean.

Look up at the beautiful sky. The clouds that were high above you are much closer now. Some are so close you can almost touch them. Not quite.

Continue floating, drifting, rising even higher if you wish.

The ground below you looks like a patchwork quilt. Green grass. Golden fields.

Yellow. Brown. Blue patches of water...rivers and lakes.

See the clouds around you. You are even able to look down on some clouds.

See the shadows they make on the ground below. Can you see the shadow from your cloud? See how the shadow drifts silently across the ground below.

Relax and luxuriate in this beautiful scene. You are so close now to another cloud above you, that if you reach out, you can touch it. What would it feel like?

You can even rise higher still, and pass right through the clouds above. Feel the mist on your cheeks as you rise through the clouds. Around you it is a glorious white, like fog...the sun shines through just enough that the white all around you glows vibrantly.

You rise higher still, suddenly coming through the clouds and into the open, dazzling sunlight shining on your face. The sky above is brilliant blue.

You can look down on the cloud you just passed, and see the white, fluffy peaks and valleys of this cloud below. It looks like perfect snow. Looking around below you it is as if you are above a land of snow. The sun shines brightly.

Lie back on your cloud, floating...relaxing...

Feel the cloud beneath you...still supporting you smoothly and comfortably.

Take your cloud wherever you wish...higher, lower, side to side...drift wherever you want to go.

Enjoy the sights around you, as you are flying wherever you wish...

(Pause)

Continue floating on the cloud, relaxing...

Imagine wherever it is you would like to go. Your cloud can take you there.

Maybe you want to float above the mountains, drifting above their rocky peaks.

Perhaps you would like to drift along the coast of the ocean, watching the waves crashing to shore.

Maybe you would like to float through the city, drifting in and out among buildings and watching the cars below.

You can travel anywhere you wish. You can look down on forests...the countryside...even your own home...float wherever you like.

(Pause)

Enjoy the sights around you. Enjoy floating on a cloud. You are so relaxed...so peaceful...

(Pause)

Now it is time to return to your day. Let your cloud take you there. Feel your cloud flying through the sky, back to where you need to go.

Let your cloud lower you down, back toward the ground. Float back to where you were when you started this visualization. Let the cloud meld with the bed, chair, or whatever surface you are on. Feel the cloud slowly disappear as the real surface becomes more solid beneath you.

Notice now your surroundings. Gradually come back to the present. Feel the surface beneath you. Hear the sounds around you. Become more and more aware and alert.

Continue to rest for a few moments longer, but open your eyes and look around. See your surroundings.

Wiggle your fingers and toes, feeling your body reawaken. Shrug your shoulders. Move your arms and legs. Turn your head.

When you are ready, you can return to your day, feeling refreshed and alert after your journey floating on a cloud.

Peaceful Place

This script will allow you to relax your mind and imagine your own safe, peaceful place. This place will be an imaginary area that you can visualize to help calm and relax your mind when you are feeling stressed.

Start reading the script here:

Begin by setting aside a few minutes so that you can relax without having anything else you need to focus on. Find a comfortable position.

For the next few moments, focus on calming your mind by focusing on your breathing. Allow your breathing to center and relax you. Breathe in...and out.

In...out...

In...out...

Continue to breathe slowly and peacefully as you allow the tension to start to leave your body.

Release the areas of tension, feeling your muscles relax and become more comfortable with each breath.

Continue to let your breathing relax you...

Breathe in...2...3...4...hold...2...3...breathe out...2...3...4...5...

Again...2...3...4...hold...2...3...out...2...3...4...5...

Continue to breathe slowly, gently, comfortably...

Let the rate of your breathing become gradually slower as your body relaxes.

Now begin to create a picture in your mind of a place where you can completely relax. Imagine what this place needs to be like in order for you to feel calm and relaxed.

Start with the physical layout of the place you are imagining...Where is this peaceful place? You might envision somewhere outdoors...or indoors...it may be a small place or large one...create an image of this place.

(Pause)

Now picture some more details about your peaceful place. Who is in this place? Are you alone? Or perhaps you are with someone else? Are there other people present? Animals? Birds? Imagine who is at your place, whether it is you only, or if you have company.

(Pause)

Imagine even more detail about your surroundings. Focus now on the relaxing sounds around you in your peaceful place.

Now imagine any tastes and smells your place has to offer.

Imagine the sensations of touch...including the temperature, any breeze that may be present, the surface you are on...imagine the details of this calming place in your mind.

Focus now on the sights of your place..colors...shapes...objects... plants...water...all of the beautiful things that make your place enjoyable.

To add further detail to this relaxing scene, imagine yourself there. What would you be doing in this calming place? Perhaps you are just sitting, enjoying this place, relaxing. Maybe you imagine walking around...or doing any other variety of activities.

Picture yourself in this peaceful place. Imagine a feeling of calm...of peace...a place where you have no worries, cares, or concerns...a place where you can simply rejuvenate, relax, and enjoy just being.

(Pause)

Enjoy your peaceful place for a few moments more. Memorize the sights, sounds, and sensations around you. Know that you can return to this place in your mind whenever you need a break. You can take a mental vacation to allow yourself to relax and regroup before returning to your regular roles.

In these last few moments of relaxation, create a picture in your mind that you will return to the next time you need a quick relaxation break. Picture yourself in your peaceful place. This moment you are imagining now, you can picture again the next time you need to relax.

When you are ready to return to your day, file away the imaginary place in your mind, waiting for you the next time you need it.

Turn your attention back to the present. Notice your surroundings as your body and mind return to their usual level of alertness and wakefulness.

Keep with you the feeling of calm from your peaceful place as you return to your everyday life.

Peaceful Meadow

This visualization script will guide you to imagine relaxing in a peaceful meadow.

Start reading the script here:

Take a moment to relax your body. Get comfortable. Notice how your body feels, and make some slight adjustments to increase your comfort. Take a deep breath in. Hold it...and breathe out, releasing tension.

Breathe in again, and as you exhale, allow your body to relax slightly.

Continue to breathe slowly...deeply.

As you visualize the following scene, let your body and mind become more and more relaxed with each moment.

Imagine yourself walking outdoors.

You are walking through the trees...small aspens, their leaves moving in a slight breeze.

The sun shines down warmly.

You walk toward a clearing in the trees. As you come closer to the clearing, you see that it is a meadow.

You walk out of the trees, into the meadow. Tall green grass blows gently...

You are probably feeling a bit tired...it would be so nice to sit down in the grass.

Walk further into the meadow now...looking around...

Imagine the meadow in your mind's eye...

What does this peaceful meadow look like?

Find a place to sit. You might want to sit or lie down in the grass...perhaps you have a blanket with you that you can unroll over the soft grass and lie down.

Feel the breeze caress your skin as you sit or lie down in the sun.

It is a pleasant day...warm, but not hot...quiet and peaceful.

Notice the sights around you. The grass, whispering...see the mix of meadow grasses, clover, wildflowers around you.

Watch a small ladybug climb a blade of grass...climbing up toward the top, pausing for a moment, and then flying away.

Imagine closing your eyes and listening to the sounds of the peaceful meadow.

Hear birds singing...the breeze rustling the grass softly...

Feel the sun on your face. Imagine turning your face up toward the sky, eyes closed, enjoying the warmth of the sun.

Smell the grass...the wildflowers...the smell of the sun on the earth ...

Look around again to see the sights around you. Notice how the ground follows gentle contours of hills. See the blue sky above you...a few wispy clouds drifting slowly by.

See the trees at the edge of the meadow.

The meadow is lush and green, a haven for birds and animals. As you watch, a deer peers out through the trees, and emerges to graze at the edge of the meadow.

The deer raises its head to look at you, sniffing the breeze, and then turns, disappearing silently into the trees.

Rest and luxuriate in this peaceful meadow. Notice the sights, sounds, and smells around you. Feel the soft grass beneath you, the sun and breeze on your skin. Imagine all the details of this place.

(Pause)

Now it is time to leave the peaceful meadow and return to the present. Notice your surroundings. Feel the surface beneath you. Hear the sounds around you.

Open your eyes to look around, reorienting yourself to the present.

Take a moment to stretch your muscles and allow your body to reawaken.

When you are ready, return to your usual activities, keeping with you a feeling of peace and calm.

Starry Sky

This starry sky relaxation is a guided visualization script that will describe relaxing at dusk and watching the stars appear in the night sky.

Start reading the script here:

Start by finding a comfortable position. As you settle in, direct your attention to your body. Notice how your body feels in this moment. Let your body begin to relax by releasing the areas of tension, such as your shoulders...feel the tension slipping away as you lower your shoulders slightly and let the muscles give up their hold.

Take a deep breath in...and as you exhale, let your body relax even more. Where is your body feeling the most tense? Focus your attention on this area as you take another breath in...and feel this area relaxing as you breathe out.

Breathe in...and out...

In...out...

Continue to take slow, deep breaths.

Where is your body the most relaxed? Notice how this area feels. Notice how the relaxation feels. See how you can let this relaxed feeling increase...growing...relaxing...feeling your whole body relax...as if your muscles are melting...softening...relaxing.

As your body relaxes more and more, you can also relax your mind as you focus on the guided imagery to follow.

Imagine that you are outdoors at dusk. It is still light out, but the sun has set below the horizon.

It is a pleasant temperature, comfortable...and you are in a safe, peaceful place in the country. Maybe you are on a farm, or in the mountains, or in the open prairie...picture a place that feels calm, safe, and serene...a place you would enjoy watching the starry sky at night.

Imagine the details of your surroundings. You are probably sitting in a chair, or lying on a blanket. Your position allows you to admire the sky above.

See the grass on the ground around you. You might see some trees, or rocks...or even just wide open plains. Imagine this pleasant scene, and feel yourself relaxing, simply enjoying this solitude.

The sky is becoming gradually darker. The highest part of the sky is a deep indigo color, becoming darker and darker as the moments pass. This color blends into a lighter shade, almost green. On the horizon, the sky is an interesting shade of pink, mixed with gray in the fading light.

It is very peaceful watching the sky darken. The air around you is still and calm. In the distance, you can hear crickets and frogs as they begin to sing.

The air is slightly cooler now, very pleasantly cool against your forehead and cheeks.

Looking at the horizon now, shapes such as distant trees or buildings are in silhouette. Your eyes are slowly adjusting to the decreasing light. As you gaze up at the sky above, it stretches from horizon to horizon like a vast dome.

Straight up above, the sky is growing darker, and is nearly black...fading to a lighter color near the horizon in the West.

You can see the first stars appear...first one star...and then another...and another...see them twinkle...shining like tiny diamonds.

As you look at the darkening sky, you can see more and more stars.

Relax and enjoy the dusk...watching night begin.

(Pause)

The sky is even darker now. It has become a dark black, with only a slight hint of light at the horizon where the sun has set. The sky is so clear...you see no clouds anywhere to obscure the starry sky.

More stars have appeared, until now the sky looks like it has been sprinkled by a salt shaker full of gleaming crystals of salt, which are the stars. Some stars are bright, luminous...others are tiny specs that you can barely see.

Simply enjoy relaxing under the starry sky...enjoying this quiet retreat.

(Pause)

Now the sky is jet black. Out here, away from city lights, the stars are amazingly bright. Have you ever seen so many stars? The sky is filled with so many stars...you would not even be able to count them.

See the constellations formed by stars...it is like hundreds of connect-the-dots pictures spread out before you. The sky is so huge...so vast...a beautiful glimmering blanket of stars stretching up in a complete circle around you from every horizon.

Admire the starry sky...feeling very calm...relaxed...at peace...

(Pause)

When you are ready to leave your imagined peaceful place, you can begin to reawaken your body and mind.

Feel your muscles reawakening as you take note of your surroundings.

Slowly return to the present...

Move your muscles by wiggling your fingers...now open and close your hands a few times.

Wiggle your toes...move your ankles...

Move your arms and legs...

Stretch if you want to...feeling your body become fully awake.

Take a moment to sit quietly as you reawaken completely. Notice that you still feel calm and relaxed, though you are awake and alert.

When your mind and body are fully awake, you can resume your usual activities, feeling refreshed.

Summer Clouds Visualization

This summer clouds relaxation script will guide you to imagine gazing at the clouds on a warm summer day.

Start reading the script here:

To begin, make yourself comfortable as you find a comfortable place to lie down.

Begin to become aware of your breathing.

Notice each breath as it goes in...and out...

Take a moment to focus your attention on your breathing, without trying to change anything. Just notice your breathing, focusing intently on each breath.

(Pause)

Now see how you can slow the rhythm of your breathing by counting. Breathe in to the count of four, hold for a count of three, and exhale to the count of five.

Breathe in...2...3...4...pause...2...3...breathe out...2...3...4...5...

Breathe in...2...3...4...hold...2...3...exhale...2...3...4...5...

Breathe in...2...3...4...pause...2...3...breathe out...2...3...4...5...

Breathe in...2...3...4...pause...2...3...exhale...2...3...4...5...

Breathe in...2...3...4...hold...2...3...exhale...2...3...4...5...

Continue to breathe slowly, smoothly...relaxing more with each breath.

Feel yourself becoming more and more relaxed.

As you relax, start to create a picture in your mind. Imagine that you are lying on a blanket outside on a warm summer day. The blanket is in the soft grass, next to some trees.

The sun shines down warmly, and a cool breeze blows across your skin.

See the sky above, blue and bright. See the clouds floating by...blowing in the breeze.

Picture in your mind the details of this scene. The feeling of the sun and breeze on your skin. The soft grass and blanket beneath you. The trees beside you, a mix of leafy trees and conifers.

The leaves on aspens and poplars wave and turn as they blow in the wind. You can hear the rustle of the leaves. Between the leaves, you can see the trunks and branches of large, old trees, empty of leaves. The bark is dark with small patches of light-colored mosses and lichens. A few spruce trees grow among the aspens. Their branches move slightly up and down, springing back as the wind blows them.

Watch the clouds passing the branches...drifting by. Notice the different shapes of clouds. Some are round, fluffy cumulus clouds. Others are long, thin, wispy clouds...like streaks of semitransparent white paint across the blue of the sky. The clouds drift lazily by. Slowly...smoothly... floating.

It is so relaxing, watching the clouds drift by in the sky above.

The sun shining down warms and relaxes you, creating a calm, sleepy feeling.

The breeze keeps you cool and comfortable.

Feel your body relaxing...bit by bit...as you sink into the soft blanket and grass beneath you.

Feel your muscles relaxing...letting go. Allow your breathing to slow as you rest peacefully.

(Pause)

Imagine the sights and sounds of this relaxing scene. The sound of the wind in the trees...birds singing. Picture the leaves of the trees as you see them moving...twisting...the sun shining through the trees...dappled on your face...

Enjoy relaxing, gazing up at the sky...watching the clouds drift by... enjoying this beautiful day.

(Pause)

When you are ready to leave this peaceful place, slowly begin to return your awareness to the present.

Take a deep breath in...and out.

Breathe in again...and out...

Continue to breathe smoothly and regularly, feeling your energy increasing with each breath.

As you breathe, allow your body to reawaken. Feel the energy flowing through your muscles.

Raise your shoulders as you breathe in, and lower them as you breathe out. Feel your muscles reawaken.

Keep with you the feeling of calm and relaxation while returning to a state of wakefulness.

When you are ready, open your eyes and return to your day, feeling alert and calm.

Peaceful Waves Relaxation

This peaceful waves relaxation script describes relaxing by the ocean at dawn while you watch the small, calm waves move rhythmically.

Start reading the script here:

It's time to relax...time to take a mental vacation. Start by making yourself comfortable. You may want to sit or lie down...loosening any tight clothing and adjusting your position so you can relax.

Begin to let go of tension and relax your body. Just start with one small area of your body that is tense. Notice this area of tension, and allow it to ease slightly.

Take a deep breath in...and as you exhale, feel the muscles in the area you are focusing on becoming more relaxed. Imagine breathing in relaxation...and breathing out tension. Notice with each breath how you can relax this one area of tension.

You may want to scan your body now for other areas of tension. Choose one area to focus on, and concentrate on breathing in relaxation...and breathing out tension. Feel your muscles relaxing...loosening...as you breathe slowly and deeply.

Notice now where your body is the most relaxed. See how this feeling of relaxation is growing...spreading...to other areas of your body...

Feel your muscles relaxing...becoming loose...your limbs are feeling heavy and relaxed...your eyelids feel very heavy.

Go ahead and close your eyes, if you haven't done so already...and as you continue to relax further, begin to create a picture in your mind.

Imagine that you are near the ocean...just before sunrise. Perhaps you are on the beach...or a hammock...or a dock. The ocean is very calm. Most of the water looks very smooth, but you can see small ripples where gentle, peaceful waves roll in toward the shore.

Take a few moments to imagine this scene.

(Pause)

Picture all the details of this relaxing place. The sun has not yet risen, but the sky is just starting to get light. The air is cool, comfortable, and pleasant. The temperature is very pleasant...a calm and comfortable morning.

Imagine the feel of a slight, gentle breeze on your skin. The breeze blows just enough to move the leaves of palm trees gently back and forth. The leaves of the trees make a dark silhouette against the gradually lightening sky.

Imagine the fresh smell of the air...the smell of the clean water and sand. It is a refreshing scent.

Picture in your mind the sound of the water lapping against the shore. The sea is so calm, the waves are very quiet, but you can hear them as they move gently and calmly.

Hear the slight rustling of leaves as the palm branches sway gently.

It is early morning, and you are the only one here. This is such a calm, safe, pleasant place. Relax here near the gentle ocean.

Perhaps you are on a deck with wooden tables...umbrellas, closed for the night. They will soon be opened to provide shelter from the sun, but for now they remain with their cloth tops folded down, as if resting.

Small huts with grass roofs provide shelter for some of the tables. During the day, this place is bustling with activity, as people sit at the tables in the shelter of the grass huts, sipping cool drinks by the water. But now, all is quiet...peaceful...serene.

Notice that the sun is starting to rise. You can see a spot of light at the horizon, as if the sun is rising right out of the water. See the light growing as the sun begins to rise above the horizon. Small streaks of light shine into the sky, as the sky grows lighter and lighter with the growing dawn.

See the birds that are active early in the morning. Some fly overhead...some are already diving into the water looking for fish. Other birds simply sit quietly.

They too are enjoying the dawn.

You can see waves as they break some distance from the shore. White peaks rise in a line out in the water, crashing on a stone breaker that keeps the water close to the shore peaceful and calm.

See the waves crashing on the breaker.

See the peaceful waves gently lapping at the shore...washing gently onto the sand.

The waves are very calming...they are so peaceful...so rhythmic.

Watch the peaceful waves flowing like your breath...in...and out...in...out...continue to observe the rhythm of the waves, flowing with the rhythm of your breath.

(Pause)

As you relax, you can enjoy the beautiful sunrise. Pink and orange give everything around you a warm glow. The sun has risen above the horizon...still low in the sky...

The breeze...the warm early sunlight...the gently lapping, peaceful waves...softly moving palm leaves...all of these create a calm and peaceful place.

Continue to relax for a few moments here...enjoying the peaceful waves and the remaining calm time at sunrise.

(Pause)

Soon this place will be busy with people going about their morning routines. Enjoy the last few remaining moments of solitude as the sun rises higher in the sky.

The sun is shining, brighter each moment. This has become a beautiful morning. You can see people in the distance, walking along the beach.

The waves become a little bigger, a bit more lively, as the breeze increases.

Everything around you seems to be waking up...getting ready for a lovely day.

When you are ready to wake up your body and your mind and return to the present, give yourself a few moments to do so.

Return your awareness to your surroundings and notice the real environment you are in.

Let your muscles wake up by opening and closing your hands, shrugging your shoulders, moving around a bit.

Keep with you the feeling of peace and calm you had while you were relaxing, as you open your eyes and sit quietly for a moment.

When you are awake and alert, you can return to your usual activities, knowing that you can return to this place in your mind whenever you want to relax.

Wildlife Sanctuary

This wildlife sanctuary relaxation script is a visualization exercise that guides you to imagine relaxing in a nature sanctuary.

Start reading the script here:

Get ready to relax your body and your mind. Settle into a comfortable position and begin to turn your attention inward.

Notice how you are feeling right now...mentally...physically. Without trying to change anything, simply take note of how your body feels... and notice how you are feeling mentally.

Mentally scan your body now, looking for areas of tension. Where is your body the most tense?

Notice now where your body is most relaxed. See that these areas of relaxation are slowly getting larger...

Now turn your awareness to your breathing. Simply notice your breathing, without making any effort to change your breathing in any way.

Imagine breathing in relaxation...and breathing out tension.

Feel yourself becoming more relaxed with each breath.

Focus in on areas of tension in your body, and imagine directing your breath to these areas. Feel the breath in drawing in relaxation...and as you exhale, imagine the tension draining away from each area of tension. Allow your breathing to relax your body.

Feel your body and mind becoming relaxed...calm...peaceful.

Deeply relaxed and calm.

Imagine that you are walking along a path...entering a wildlife sanctuary. This sanctuary is a preserved nature area...maybe in the wilderness, or perhaps in the middle of a city.

The path is paved...just wide enough for walking. Enter the wildlife sanctuary, walking along the path. Wild grass grows beside the path, and there are trees on both sides.

Birds are singing off in the distance.

It is a beautiful, sunny day. The air is pleasant and warm, a slight breeze making it even more comfortable. Feel the sun shining down on you... warming and relaxing your body.

Take a deep breath, enjoying the fresh air. Breathe out, feeling invigorated.

Take another deep breath in...and out...

Continue to breathe the fresh, clean air.

The path curves up ahead, continuing deeper into the beautiful wildlife sanctuary.

As you continue along the path, you admire the scene around you. Small trees grow near the path, their bark smooth and light colored... small round leaves twisting gently in the breeze.

Further back from the path, larger trees grow....see the variety of trees.

Wildflowers grow in the grass right next to the path.

As you round a curve in the path, you can see ahead of you a clearing... it is a pond, or a small lake.

You can see up ahead that the path continues next to the water.

As you walk toward the water, the sun shines down, birds sing, a breeze blows...it is so peaceful here...such a beautiful day. You feel very content.

Continue to walk toward the pond, seeing the reeds growing among the grass near the water. As you approach the pond, you can hear even more birds singing. Getting closer to the water, you see the reeds getting thicker toward the water's edge and continuing around the shallow edges of the pool. The deeper water toward the center is smooth.

See the ducks swimming...leaving small wakes behind them...the water flowing out in a V shape as the birds slowly swim through the water.

As you continue along the path, you walk beside the pond, enjoying the sights and sounds of this wildlife sanctuary.

Up ahead, the paved trail connects with a wooden path, like a dock, that extends over the water and to a bird watching blind. This would be a wonderful place to sit.

Imagine yourself continuing along the paved trail, approaching the wooden path.

You can see more birds now, black birds with red wings darting in and out of the reeds. Geese. Loons. Sparrows. Chickadees.

A muskrat swims among the reeds, then dives under the water.

You are almost to the wooden path now. Step onto this path if you wish, walking above the reeds and the mud at the sides of the pond... now over reeds and water. The blind is located right in the middle of the reeds, but above them, so you are directly among the birds.

The blind has wooden sides, with openings that you can look through, and inside this structure there are comfortable benches where you can relax. The sides go slightly higher than the top of your head, and the top of the blind is open to the sky.

Imagine sitting on a bench, and closing your eyes for a moment to simply enjoy the sun and the peaceful sounds of the wildlife around you.

(Pause)

Look around now, at the beautiful scenery around you. The sanctuary is such a calm, serene treed area with this lake in the middle. Imagine peering through the window of the blind...look out over the water, admiring it's stillness...reflecting the blue sky and a few small white clouds. Across the water, in the distance, are more trees...and beyond that, a grassy, green hill.

This scene makes a perfect picture, with water, trees, hills, and sky...

Imagine looking out of another opening in the blind, looking a different direction. Look out across the reeds...along the edge of the pond. See as a deer emerges from the trees to drink from the pond, delicately stepping through the reeds to water. See the water dripping from its muzzle as the deer raises its head. The deer turns and disappears back into the trees.

Another muskrat swims by.

A colorful duck flies overhead, and spreads its wings to descend and land in the water. Water sprays and splashes out to the sides of the duck as its feet skim the surface, before finally lowering its body, folding its wings, and swimming. Another duck follows, landing in the water to swim alongside the first one.

A small bird lands right on the top edge of the blind, and looks at you, chirping pleasantly. The bird stays for a few moments before flying off.

Relax in this peaceful wildlife sanctuary. You may want to imagine lying back and closing your eyes, or continuing to look around. Imagine spending time however you wish, here in this peaceful place.

(Pause)

You are so relaxed and calm.

At peace...content.

Relax for a few moments longer in this wildlife sanctuary.

You are feeling calm and relaxed, and you can return to this state whenever you need to in order to feel calm and at peace.

Keep with you this feeling of relaxation while you slowly return your awareness to the present.

Keeping your eyes closed for a few moments longer, notice the surface you are on. Notice the feeling of your clothing against your skin.

Turn your attention to the sounds of your environment around you.

Feel your mind and body reawaken as your awareness of your surroundings increases.

Open your eyes, looking around you at your surroundings. Become fully aware of the environment around you.

When you have returned to your usual level of alertness, you can return to your day feeling awake, calm, and relaxed.

Get Rid of Nightmares

Many people experience night terrors and struggle with how to get rid of nightmares. This relaxation script uses guided imagery and visualization to help return your mind to a peaceful, restful state free of fear after experiencing a nightmare.

Start reading the script here:

Let's begin the relaxation exercise. Perhaps you have just had a nightmare...or maybe you are getting ready to sleep and want to fill your mind with peaceful images...or perhaps you have woken up in the night and want to get back to sleep. Maybe you just want to promote positive mental images to help you relax. Whatever the case may be, this relaxation exercise can help to create a peaceful mental state.

Positive images can help to get rid of nightmares.

This guided imagery will help eliminate nightmares and create a positive place in your mind. Positive visualization can create this place.

Imagine a place that is perfectly safe, and very comfortable. Imagine what this place would be like. Create an image in your mind of all the details of a safe, peaceful place.

With this image in mind, begin to relax your body. Fear creates tension, and to get rid of nightmares it is important to decrease this tension. Start by noticing where the tension is in your body. Pay close attention to your shoulders, neck, back, hands, and jaw. These are areas where tension tends to build up.

Once you have located the tension in your body, choose one area to relax first. Focus your attention on this area, and consciously allow the muscles to relax and soften, becoming loose. Breathe, imagining that your breath brings relaxation to this area. Feel the tension leave as you breathe out.

Breathe in relaxation...and breathe out tension. Keep breathing, letting your breaths be slow and regular.

Notice that the area you were focusing on is more relaxed than it was before. See how you have the ability to relax your muscles.

Feel your muscles relaxing further. Notice your jaw relaxing, becoming loose, your mouth resting comfortably with your teeth slightly apart. Feel your neck and shoulders relaxing and your shoulders getting lower as the muscles give up their hold.

Allow your hands to relax, resting...open, loose, relaxed.

Feel your back relax. All the muscles become soft and loose.

To get rid of nightmares, let's create a positive image to focus on.

Imagine that you are at a luxurious resort where you are completely safe and cared for. Your room is spacious, sunny, and comfortable.

In this place, you have no worries. There is nothing you need to do. You are here just to relax and take time for yourself.

The room you are staying in is very luxurious. You have a large space with everything you need...kitchen, bathroom, bedroom, living room. Picture being in a large room that is just for relaxation and enjoyment. This room is your own private escape. Here is a warm pool, a soft, comfortable lounge chair, plants, and large windows. The sun streams through the windows, making the pool sparkle.

Take in this scene, imagining this lovely place. Though this room is indoors, the plants and pool create an almost outdoor feel. Through the windows, you can see a beautiful view.

Imagine where your resort is located. What do you see outside? Your resort can be anywhere you like...by the ocean, in the mountains, on a golf course, an oasis in the desert...wherever you want your resort to be. Imagine the picturesque view you would see out the windows.

The room is warm, with a soft breeze created by silent fans. Imagine yourself here, in this safe, luxurious, beautiful place. You may see yourself walking toward the pool, or perhaps sitting in the lounge chair. Here you can do whatever you wish.

I'll pause for one minute. For the next minute, imagine the relaxing things you can do here, and create a picture in your mind of you relaxing in this peaceful place.

(Pause)

Now imagine resting on the lounge chair. Feel the sun shining down as you become warm and relaxed. The chair is very soft, and as you recline, lying back and closing your eyes, you feel very at peace.

You are so comfortable here. Feel yourself sinking into the lounge chair, sinking deeper into relaxation.

Notice the peaceful thoughts that are filling your mind. See that by focusing on these thoughts, they become stronger...filling your consciousness with peace. The peaceful thoughts are very clear... increasing in clarity as you focus.

All other thoughts and concerns are far away right now. As you sleep, your mind can remain in this positive place. Feel yourself drifting off to sleep, filled with peaceful, pleasant thoughts. Beautiful, serene dreams occupy your consciousness.

Calm...peace...relaxed...

Thoughts that enter your awareness can pass lazily through your mind, like clouds drifting by...you don't need to focus especially on any of them. You are so calm. Allow your thoughts to pass without dwelling on them. You can get rid of nightmares by allowing the negative images and thoughts to leave your mind, as they are replaced by images of the peaceful resort in your imagination.

Turn your attention again to the pool and lounge chair you imagined. See this peaceful place, just for you. Only pleasant thoughts remain here. This place is a retreat from all stresses and worries.

Any time worried thoughts arise, focus again on the resort...a luxurious, safe place where you can get away from life's stresses, get rid of nightmares, and just relax. See all the details of this place. You can picture yourself enjoying the pool and sun room...or having a warm bath in a jacuzzi tub. Perhaps you imagine getting into a large, soft, comfortable bed and having a nap. Your suite has a variety of things for you to enjoy, and it is a place just for you, where you can relax.

Relax here...resting...enjoying this holiday. Fill your mind with happiness and peace.

(Pause)

Now, if you want to, you can drift off to sleep...ever so slowly drifting down into a pleasant, calm land of dreams.

Slipping deeper and deeper...

I'll count now from one to five. When you reach five you will be fully relaxed and asleep.

One...becoming heavier, sleepy and relaxed.

Two...safe and warm, comfortably floating...drifting...relaxed

Three...pleasant, peaceful, happy thoughts fill your mind

Four...so deeply relaxed...

Five...drifting into a deep sleep, filled with pleasant dreams.

Tropical Paradise

It is time to relax...time to take a mental vacation to a tropical paradise where you can enjoy the beach, nature, and sunshine.

As you start to relax, begin to become aware of your breathing.

Notice each breath as it goes in...and out...

See how you can slow the rhythm of your breathing by counting. Breathe in to the count of 4, hold for a count of 3, and exhale to the count of 5.

Breathe in...2...3...4...hold...2...3...exhale...2...3...4...5...

Breathe in...2...3...4...hold...2...3...exhale...2...3...4...5...

Breathe in...2...3...4...hold...2...3...exhale...2...3...4...5...

Breathe in...2...3...4...hold...2...3...exhale...2...3...4...5...

Breathe in...2...3...4...hold...2...3...exhale...2...3...4...5...

Continue to breathe slowly, smoothly...relaxing more with each breath.

Feel yourself becoming more and more relaxed.

As your body relaxes...and your mind becomes more calm...start to create a picture in your mind. Your vacation begins in a tropical jungle, at a waterfall. Hear the water cascading down the rocks into a perfectly clear pool.

Imagine standing next to the pool, admiring the cascade of water coming down from the rocky shelf above.

Trees and vines surround the pool, growing luxuriously in the moist soil around the pool and stream.

Hear the birds around you in the trees. There are many friendly birds and animals in the trees around you.

The air around you is very warm, and the mist from the waterfall feels pleasantly cool on your skin.

Look around you to see the lush vegetation and the wildlife here. Parrots. Toucans. Monkeys. Iguanas. Colorful butterflies. A variety of animals quietly move in the trees, as near or as far away as makes you comfortable.

Notice the vegetation here. Trees, vines, flowers. Very lush and green. Notice the fresh smell of the air, with the scent of flowers, trees, and mist.

Imagine the things you can do to relax here in this tropical paradise. You could swim in the pool, even climb to the top of the waterfall and dive into the pool below.

Enjoy relaxing at this jungle waterfall.

(Pause)

Now imagine walking along a path that leads away from the waterfall and pool. Looking ahead, you can see clear blue sky through a break in the trees.

You can see the brilliant blue of the ocean ahead. Hear the waves crashing to shore, though you cannot yet see the waves, only the color of the ocean between the trees.

The path you are walking on is sandy...soft, white sand.

As you walk toward the ocean, you emerge from the jungle onto a sandy area filled with palm trees.

You can see the waves crashing to shore now, washing up on rocks and coral. Each wave that hits the rocks on the shore splashes high into the air.

The air is very clean, and smells of clean ocean water and sand warmed by the sun.

Walk along the sand, if you like, through the palm trees, parallel to the shore. The waves crash to the shore beside you.

As you walk along the shore line, the rocks and coral become fewer and the waves wash up onto the sand.

Ahead of you is a stretch of white sand.

The sun shines on the water, bringing out a brilliant blue...the brightest blue you have ever seen.

Where the water is shallow, washing onto the sand, it is turquoise blue. Going out from the shore, the water deepens in color to a deep, brilliant sapphire blue.

Imagine walking out along the white sand, down to the edge of the water. Pause for a moment, standing in the hot, white sand, to look out across the water. Further down the beach, rocky cliffs meet the ocean. The waves crash into the rocks, splashing.

A huge, tall rock stands out in the water, like an island.

The sand before you is smooth and white and very soft. It feels so soft against your feet. Walk toward the water...until you reach the damp sand where the waves wash up on shore. This damp sand is firm and cool. Enjoy the feeling of coolness on your feet.

The hot sun is shining down...a cool breeze touches your skin, providing relief from the heat.

Walk along the water's edge...waves wash up, washing over the tops of your feet, and then receding.

Walk along the water, toward the rocky cliffs, along this pristine white beach. As you approach the cliffs, you see a group of palm trees, with a hut that has a grass roof. Beside the hut is a hammock, stretching between two palm trees, gently swaying in the breeze.

Approach the hut and hammock, if you want to...inside the hut are towels...fruit...and a tall glass of ice water, just for you.

Imagine relaxing at this beautiful place, enjoying the food, water, sunshine, and shade...the sand and the ocean...your own tropical paradise.

Do whatever it is you would like to do...enjoying this place...

(Pause)

You are feeling relaxed...a bit tired...imagine how nice it would feel to lie in the hammock. The hammock is in dappled shade...the sun filtering through the leaves of palm trees. Imagine lying in the hammock...

The hammock sways gently...

Look up at the swaying palm leaves...you can see bits of the blue sky between the leaves...small clouds floating by...

Rest in the hammock...relaxing...the breeze blowing across your skin... relax...

You are so calm...so relaxed...peaceful...relaxed.

(Pause)

Now it is time to leave your picture. Before you reawaken your mind and body, take a moment to remember this tropical paradise, a place you can return to in your imagination when you want to relax.

Slowly return to the present...gradually becoming aware of the sounds around you...noticing where you are...

Move your muscles a little, allowing your body to reawaken.

Open your eyes and look around you, taking in your environment as you become more alert.

When you are fully awake and alert you can return to your usual activities, keeping with you a feeling of calm.

Hot Springs Relaxation

This hot springs relaxation will guide you to imagine relaxing outdoors in a natural hot water spring in the mountains.

Start by finding a comfortable position, seated or lying down. Let your arms rest at your sides, with your hands open, limp and relaxed.

Breathe deeply and slowly to start to relax your body. Breathe in...and out.

In...out.

In...out.

Keep breathing slowly like this, allowing each breath to relax your body as you release tension each time you exhale.

Create a picture in your mind of a quiet retreat in the mountains. Right now you are in a cozy cabin.

Out the windows you can see the snowy landscape. The cabin is on a mountainside, and is surrounded by trees and rocks.

Looking out the window, you can see huge rocks, towering above the cabin. Between a crack in the rocks, you can see a trickle of steaming water. The snow all around this trickle of water is melted, exposing the gray rocks to either side. The water flows down into a natural pool.

Imagine that you are wearing sandals and a warm bathrobe over a bathing suit, preparing to go out to the hot springs.

Picture opening the front door of the cabin, and stepping out into the snow.

As you walk briskly along the path, some of the snow touches the top of your bare feet. It is so cold, you feel a tingly, almost burning sensation where the snow touched your skin.

You rush toward the water, seeing the steam rising from the hot springs. There is so much steam, the air around you is foggy.

You reach the side of the hot springs, where the hot water has melted the snow all around. The springs are perfectly clear, and made of rock.

The water at the side of the springs is shallow. Imagine stepping out of your bath robe, and laying it on the warm, dry rocks where the snow has melted. You step out of your shoes and into the steaming water.

The water at the edge of the pool is ankle deep. After the feeling of the cold snow, the water feels very hot on your feet.

The air around you is cold, and snow flakes are falling softly.

To get relief from the cold, you step further into the hot springs. The rocks make natural seats in the water. You can sit down in the water, which comes up to just below your chin.

Feel the luxurious warmth all around you. Your hands and feet feel tingly and hot at first...eventually settling into a pleasant feeling of warmth.

The water is just the right temperature. Your feet rest on the smooth rock bottom of the hot springs, and you can lean back against the gently sloped stone sides of the pool.

Imagine leaning back and closing your eyes with a sigh.

Allow your body to completely relax. The warmth of the water surrounds you...

Let your arms rest at your sides, floating just a little...allow the muscles of your arms to relax completely. Your arms feel heavy and relaxed...and at the same time, weightless. It is such a calm, pleasant feeling.

Feel your neck and shoulders relaxing...surrounded by warmth. The healing water brings relaxation and calm.

Your shoulders lower slightly, relaxing, easing the tension away... becoming loose and relaxed.

Feel your upper back relaxing...your collar bones, and chest...

You are so relaxed. You can feel the water against your skin. Gently moving. Feel the occasional bubble tickle your skin as it brushes against you while it rises to the surface of the water.

Allow your stomach and lower back to relax...letting go of tension. So warm and relaxed.

Feel your legs relaxing, all the way from your hips...to your knees...to your feet. Your legs are so warm and relaxed. Like your arms, your legs feel heavy, but also weightless as they float slightly in the water.

Feel the warmth all around you. The hot springs sooth your muscles. You can relax completely.

Feel the coolness of the snow flakes on your forehead. It feels so pleasant, a wonderful contrast from the hot water.

Let all your stresses escape, drifting away like the rising steam.

(Pause)

Notice the beautiful scenery around you. Snow, trees, and rocks peering through the fog.

It is so quiet here. The only sound is the quiet trickling of the water from a crack in the rocks. You can hear the water, very quiet, as it flows into the pool.

So peaceful.

Feel your muscles relaxing even further. You are completely warm... deeply relaxed.

Just relax now, enjoying these beautiful hot springs.

(Pause)

When you are ready to reawaken and return to the hours ahead, imagine stepping out of the hot springs, onto the warm, dry rocks beside the water.

See yourself putting on your bath robe and sandals, and going back inside the cabin.

The snow that touches your feet feels pleasantly cool, and helps you to wake up.

Imagine opening the cabin door, and going inside. The cabin is warm and dry.

Keep with you a feeling of warmth and calm, as you gradually return to the present.

Notice your actual surroundings, and become reoriented to where you are right now.

Move your arms and legs, and feel your muscles waking up.

Sit quietly for a moment with your eyes open, returning to full wakefulness.

When you are completely awake and alert, you can return to your day, filled with energy.

Guided Imagery Scripts

Self-Esteem Relaxation

Relax with affirmations, meditation, visualization, and deep breathing. This self-esteem relaxation can be used to promote positive self-image and help you fall asleep in a positive frame of mind.

Begin reading the self-esteem relaxation script here:

Find a comfortable position sitting or lying down. Notice how you are feeling right now...physically and mentally.

Take a deep breath in through your nose, and release the breath through your mouth.

Take another breath...and allow your breathing to relax you as you exhale fully.

Breathe in gently...and as you breathe out, let the air carry the tension out of your body.

Continue to breathe slowly and gently as you begin to focus on relaxing your body.

Notice where your body is tense. Focus your attention on one of these areas. As you breathe, picture this part of your body becoming slightly more relaxed than it was before. With each breath, this part of your body becomes a little more relaxed.

Imagine what the relaxation feels like...tingly...soft...gentle...calm... loose...free...and let that feeling of relaxation grow.

Scan your body for any areas of tension, and for each area, let the relaxation soften the muscles as they give up their hold. Let the feeling of relaxation grow...spreading a feeling of calm throughout your body.

Breathe in relaxation...and breathe out tension...breathe in calm...and let go of all the tension as you exhale...

Continue to breathe slowly and gently, deepening your state of relaxation more and more with each breath...deeper and deeper.....more and more relaxed. Calm. At peace.

Now begin to create a picture in your mind. Imagine a place where you feel completely at ease. This might be a favorite place you have been, or somewhere you have seen, or it might be completely imaginary. It's up to you. Picture this place where you feel happy and calm.

Create the details about this place in your mind. Visualize the sights... sounds...and smells...of your place. Imagine how you feel physically. You are comfortable, enjoying the pleasant temperature... enjoying being still and relaxing or doing whatever enjoyable activities you participate in here...

Enjoy the way you feel in this safe place.

You feel calm and safe here...at peace with yourself.

Remain in your peaceful place while you meditate calmly and build your self-esteem.

Imagine that all the following affirmations are true for you, right now in this moment, and enjoy the self-esteem relaxation you experience. Repeat each affirmation in your mind, or out loud, with conviction. Use your imagination to fully believe each affirmation.

The affirmations begin now.

I am at peace with myself.

I appreciate who I am.

I value myself as a person.

All people have value, and I am a valuable human being.

I deserve to relax.

I deserve to be happy.

I embrace my happy feelings and enjoy being content.

I imagine and believe that all of these affirmations are true for me, right now in this moment, and enjoy the self-esteem and relaxation I am experiencing.

When my mood is low, I accept my emotions and recognize that the low mood will pass and I will be happy again. I look forward to the good times. My future is bright and positive.

I look forward to the future, and I enjoy the present.

I look fondly upon many memories from my past.

I forgive myself for my mistakes. All people make mistakes. I used to feel regret about some of my mistakes because I am a good person and want to do the best that I can, and now, I am still a good person and I release the feelings of regret because I have learned and moved on.

I forgive myself for errors I have made, because I have felt bad about them long enough. I have suffered enough, and now it is time to be free. By freeing myself from past mistakes, I can move on and do good things. I forgive myself.

I feel good about who I am today.

I accept the person that I am. I accept my flaws, and accept my strengths.

I view my shortcomings as strengths not yet developed rather than as weaknesses.

I eagerly develop new strengths.

I approach challenges with strength.

I do the best that I can at the time. I give 100% effort when I am able and when I choose to put full effort toward the things that are important. I accept my imperfections and the imperfections in what I do. My efforts are good enough, and they're okay.

I do not have to be perfect to be okay as a person.

I am a human being with flaws. I enjoy being who I am, and love myself as I am.

I nurture the child within me.

I feel secure in who I am, and do not need to compare myself to others.

All the strengths I have ever had are present in me today. I still have the same positive character, even if not all of my strengths are shown right now. I have all of those strengths of character, and will use those strengths again.

I imagine and believe that all of these affirmations are true for me, right now in this moment.

I accept myself.

I care for myself.

I take time for myself, and enjoy it. I deserve time for myself, and I feel good about taking this time regularly.

I handle difficulties with grace.

I allow myself to experience and express emotions, both negative and positive.

I accept myself.

I am perfectly alright just the way I am.

I accept myself.

I am a valuable human being.

I accept myself.

I feel confident.

I accept myself.

I feel secure.

I accept myself.

I accept myself.

Think again about your peaceful place. Picture yourself enjoying this environment. Acknowledge the feelings you are experiencing after repeating the self-esteem relaxation affirmations. Accept any positive or negative feelings you are having. Allow yourself to feel calm and at peace.

(Pause)

Now it is time to leave your special place. Know that you can return here in your imagination any time to relax, feel calm and relaxed, and feel comfortable and safe.

Take with you the feelings of acceptance of yourself, and belief in the self-esteem relaxation affirmations. Continue to feel positive and accepting of yourself. Hold onto this secure feeling of self-esteem as you return to your day.

In a moment I will count to three. If you choose to sleep, you can drift into a relaxing and pleasant sleep on the count of three. If you wish to become fully awake, you can increase your alertness and become energized and fully alert on the count of three.

One...take a deep, cleansing breath in...and exhale slowly.

Two...take another deep breath...and exhale...

Three...you are feeling calm, confident, and refreshed.

Healing Relaxation

This healing relaxation begins with passive progressive muscle relaxation, and then guides you to imagine your body healing itself.

Begin reading the script here:

Begin by finding a comfortable, relaxed position.

Allow your body to begin to relax.

Breathe in...and out...

Take a cleansing breath in...and breathe out the tension in your body...

Feel relaxation beginning at the bottom of your feet. It might feel like stepping into a warm bathtub...or it may feel like a tingling sensation...or simply calm and loose. Allow the relaxation to spread over your feet, and up to your ankles.

Feel the relaxation rising above your ankles, flowing up your lower legs...to your knees...continuing up to your upper legs...

Allow the relaxation to continue to spread throughout your body, rising now to your hips and pelvic area...

To your stomach and lower back...

To your chest and upper back...

Let your upper arms relax...your elbows...lower arms...and wrists...feel the relaxation spread to your hands...relaxing the palms of your hands...the back of your hands...each finger and thumb...your hands feel pleasantly warm, heavy, and relaxed.

Feel your body relaxing further as the area by your collar bones widens and relaxes...allow your shoulders to ease back slightly...

Allow your upper back to relax even further...let your shoulders relax...and your neck...

Feel the relaxation continue to spread to your chin...the back of your head...your mouth...your cheeks...nose...eyes...

Feel your eyelids, heavy and relaxed...

Notice your eyebrows relaxing...your ears relaxing...and your forehead...

Your forehead feels cool and relaxed...

Let the relaxation spread further...to the top of your head...

Your entire body now is relaxed and calm. Feel the relaxation flowing throughout your body, from your head to your feet.

You can relax even further as you let your spine relax completely. Starting where the top of your spine meets your head, feel the relaxation...feel the muscles giving up their hold and relaxing...

Feel the relaxation spread down your spine...down your neck...upper back...middle back...and lower back...all the way down to your tailbone at the bottom of your spine...

Notice all the muscles of your back relaxing completely...

Feel the relaxation flowing throughout your body.

Breathe in...now hold that breath...and relax your muscles totally, allowing the breath to flow gently out your nose or mouth.

Take another deep breath, breathing in relaxation...and release the breath. Breathe out any remaining tension.

Continue to breathe smoothly and slowly as you mentally scan your body, looking for any remaining tension.

If you notice any tension, focus on that area. Direct the relaxation to flow into that area, and then carry the tension away.

Imagine that the air you are breathing can cleanse your body and remove tension. Imagine that each breath in carries relaxation. Picture the tension in your body leaving with each breath out.

Now simply relax, calmly, enjoying the feeling of relaxation for a few moments.

(Pause)

Focus your attention now on your body, and think about the healing that needs to take place.

Create an image in your mind of your current state of being. Imagine the physical ailment that troubles you. It might be pain, or illness, or injury. It might be something diagnosed, or it may be a problem that is not yet identified. Whatever it is that you would like to heal, imagine this problem in your mind right now.

Focus on the specific location in your body where this problem is present.

You might want to imagine the problem as a dark area, and picture the healing relaxation as light. See the light of relaxation flowing through your body. Direct the light of healing relaxation toward the dark area.

Your body has many ways of healing itself. See the healing relaxation promoting your immune system...promoting strength...promoting growth of healthy tissue...removing unhealthy matter from your body... removing toxins, bacteria, or waste...cleaning up your body...

Imagine the light of healing relaxation flowing, swirling, touching the edges of the dark problem area in your body.

You might notice small pieces of the dark area being carried away by the healing relaxation...allow these dark pieces to leave your body as you breathe out.

Breathe in health, healing, and calm...

Breathe out tension, illness, and any problems in your body...

Allow the light healing relaxation to continue swirling around the dark problem area...see the dark area getting smaller...

Imagine the dark area completely enveloped by relaxation...

See the healing relaxation making the dark area lighter...and lighter... carrying away anything that is not good for your body...

Imagine your immune system working to heal you...picture the cells you need going to the places they need to go...working as needed to heal your body...

Imagine the healing relaxation flowing, coursing through your body...

Picture your body entirely filled with relaxation...

See the problem area your body is healing...see it becoming even lighter...filled with relaxation...carrying away any discomfort...healing...

Allow your body to heal itself...

Take a cleansing breath in...and breathe out what your body does not need...

Breathe in relaxation...breathe out all the old air...

Relax for a few moments and imagine the healing process going on inside your body...feeling confident in your body's ability to heal... feeling calm and at peace...

(Pause)

Now you can choose either to return to your usual level of wakefulness and alertness, or to drift into sleep.

If you choose to awaken, feel your body and mind becoming more aware of your surroundings.

If you decide to sleep, let the relaxation deepen.

I will count to three. When I reach three, you will be at your desired level of relaxation or alertness.

One...

Two...

Three.

Public Speaking Visualization

This public speaking visualization is a guided imagery script using visualization to allow you to imagine yourself calmly and successfully speaking in public.

Begin reading the script here:

To begin, choose a comfortable position, seated or lying down. Make sure that you have no distractions around you and are not trying to do anything besides focusing on these words and allowing yourself to become relaxed.

Get comfortable, preparing to relax. Start to relax your body.

Take a deep breath in...and breathe out...

In...and out...

Continue to breathe deeply, slowly, and comfortably.

I'll count down now, from ten...to one. As I say each number, you can become more relaxed.

Let's begin.

Ten...feeling your muscle start to relax...

Nine...your hands and feet are warming and relaxing...

Eight...your muscles are becoming loose and heavy...

Seven...notice your attention drifting...you are becoming more relaxed...

Six...relaxing even further now...peaceful...

Five...a tingly feeling of relaxation spreading through your body... pleasant and relaxed...

Four...further relaxed and peaceful...

Three...free of tension...

Two...almost completely relaxed now...

One...you are now deeply relaxed.

Very deeply relaxed and comfortable.

Allow this feeling of relaxation to grow...becoming even more relaxed... calm and peaceful.

Keep with you the feeling of relaxation as you think about public speaking. Notice your reaction, physically and emotionally, to the idea of public speaking. Perhaps in the past this has been a source of anxiety for you...notice now how you can be relaxed and calm while thinking about speaking in public.

Calm and relaxed.

Peaceful and relaxed.

In the future you will know that the stress symptoms you may experience when faced with speaking publicly indicate excitement. This is a positive feeling, filling you with energy. The thought of speaking in front of people fills you with good feelings of excitement and anticipation.

You may even be feeling a bit excited now, just thinking about public speaking. Let this feeling subside as you return to a state of deep relaxation.

Take a deep breath in...hold...and exhale.

Breathe in...and out.

In...out...

Continue to breathe deeply, noticing how you relax a bit more each time you exhale.

Breathe in...and relax, breathing out.

In...relax...

Breathe...relax...

Keep breathing slowly and calmly. You can relax like this any time you need to. Whenever you want to calm down, you can breathe deeply, and relax...like you are relaxing now.

(Pause)

Now let's begin a guided imagery exercise to allow you to imagine successfully speaking in public and enjoying the positive experience.

In this visualization, imagine that everything goes perfectly. Imagine what it would be like to be the most confident, best public speaker in the world.

Create an image in your mind of an excellent public speaker...imagine a confident, well spoken person...see that this person is you. Picture yourself as a superb public speaker.

Begin to create a mental picture of yourself preparing to give a speech. Imagine that you are preparing in advance to speak. You are feeling confident, excited...you're looking forward to speaking.

After your focused preparation, you are ready to speak. When the day arrives for you to do public speaking, you are excited, eager to begin.

Imagine going to the location where you will speak. See yourself looking forward to speaking. You are excited, eager to talk in public. You can't wait to share your knowledge. You have memorized the words easily, and know that they will come to you exactly as you need them.

Picture entering the location where you will speak...maybe it is an auditorium...or another place. Many people are gathered to see you. You love it. They can't wait to hear what you are going to say, and you can't wait to tell them.

Imagine getting up to the front of the room, ready to speak. The crowd waits expectantly.

Picture all the details of this scene. See yourself standing at the front of the room, feeling confident. See the people in front of you, waiting to hear you speak.

Imagine yourself beginning your speech...confident. Your phrases and words are well timed. Throughout your speech, you are breathing calmly, deeply...pausing between each sentence.

You maintain a comfortable, smooth rhythm. You talk with smooth, clear speech. Ideas flow. Your hard work and extensive preparation allow your public speaking to be easy, automatic, almost by rote. Everything seems so familiar. It is such a great feeling.

Imagine giving your speech. See yourself as you enjoy this moment. You are confident, comfortable, and having a great time. The anticipatory excitement you felt at the beginning has smoothed into a feeling of confidence and calm.

You feel so at home in front of all these people. They listen, enjoying hearing you speak as much as you are enjoying speaking. You enjoy this experience immensely.

When you reach your conclusion and speak the final words of your prepared speech, imagine giving the audience time to ask questions. You answer every question easily and proficiently. See your excellent answers satisfying each member of the audience.

The audience is pleased with your performance. You are pleased with your performance. The exhilaration at having completed this public speaking fills you with happiness, contentment, and pride. It feels great to have done this. You are even a little bit disappointed it is over because you enjoyed it so much.

Notice how you can feel confident and calm when doing public speaking. This includes giving prepared speeches, responding to questions, talking spontaneously to strangers...you are skilled and able to do any sort of public speaking.

You are able to relax before, during, or after you speak. You are confident and assertive.

Practicing this visualization in your mind is like performing actual public speaking. If you are able to do this visualization and be calm, you can also speak in public calmly. Congratulate yourself for completing this challenge.

Now that you have completed this public speaking guided imagery, take a few moments to reawaken your mind and body...gradually becoming more alert.

I'll count to five. When I reach five, you will be fully awake and feeling calm and energized.

Five...becoming more awake and alert...

Two...feeling your mind and body reawaken...

Three...move your muscles a little...

Four...almost completely awake now...

Five...feeling full of energy and refreshed.

Overcoming Shyness

This relaxation script is for overcoming shyness. Use guided imagery, affirmations, and visualization to foster a sense of self-confidence and help decrease social anxiety.

Begin reading the script here:

Start by getting comfortable. For the moment, keep your eyes open and your gaze fixed on one spot in the room. Find a position seated or lying down, and rest your arms at your sides.

Take a deep breath in...and exhale slowly.

Breathe in again...and out.

In...out.

In...out.

Keep breathing slowly, smoothly.

Allow your body to begin to relax. The first thing you might notice is that your muscles begin to let go of some of the tension they were holding. Feel your shoulders easing downward, relaxing and giving up all the tension. Your arms are feeling heavy...getting heavier...and heavier...and they pull downward gently, moving your shoulders even lower, into a loose, relaxed position.

As you relax, you may notice your eyelids starting to feel heavy. Very heavy...each blink becoming slow...moving the heaviness of your eyelids...until opening your eyes becomes an effort. It would feel so good to close your eyes...go ahead and relax, allowing your eyes to close.

Notice the rest of your body relaxing. Your legs are very heavy...so heavy and limp. Allow the muscles of your neck and back to relax. Let your hands and your feet relax. Relax your head and face.

Focus your attention for a moment on the center of your body. Let a feeling of relaxation grow, feeling the relaxation in your chest and stomach. Each breath you take can relax you even more...filling your lungs with relaxation.

Sit quietly for a moment, relaxing...letting the relaxation deepen as you breathe slowly and smoothly.

(Pause)

Start to create an image in your mind. Imagine yourself feeling confident, interacting with others positively. What would it be like if you were very confident? Imagine how you would behave...how you would carry yourself. See in your mind your confident facial expression...your self-assured posture...

How would this "confident you" behave? Imagine yourself being completely confident and not feeling shy. See yourself feeling calm and confident.

Now focus for a moment on relaxation. Turn your attention to your breathing, and feel yourself becoming more relaxed with each breath.

Take a calming breath in...and breathe slowly out...

Breathe in...and out.

Feel yourself relaxing more with each breath as you keep breathing slowly and calmly.

Turn your attention now to a situation in which you would need to interact with others. See your confident self in this situation...feeling good.

Imagine all the details...see yourself talking to others. Notice your slow, steady heart rate. See how steady your hands are and how smooth your voice is. See yourself smiling, calm, speaking out loud to individuals or groups...it feels good to imagine yourself handling all kinds of social situations positively.

(Pause)

Now change the visualization slightly to imagine the shyness itself. Picture what it is like to be shy. What does shyness mean to you? Perhaps shyness means a difficulty speaking to others. Maybe it is a feeling of embarrassment in public, or a tendency to be quiet around people. Think of what it means to you to be shy.

(Pause)

You can overcome shyness. The most effective way to overcome shyness is to challenge the shyness by facing head on the situations that are the most difficult. Picture your most difficult situation...the one in which you experience the most shyness.

You can practice facing this situation in your imagination, and then you can face this situation in real life. You will be able to handle the situation positively, with confidence, and overcome shyness.

Walk yourself through the situation now in your mind. Picture as many details as you can...and see yourself handling the challenge, facing directly the situation in which you feel the most shy.

Picture the confident self you were imagining a few moments ago, and see yourself facing a situation where you felt shy in the past. See yourself overcoming shyness.

It's okay if you feel nervous...this feeling of nervousness will go away as soon as you see how capable you are. You are stronger and more capable of overcoming shyness than you may realize. Take a few moments now to mentally face the situation in which you experience the most shyness.

(Pause)

Imagine your future self...a self that is not shy. See that this same person is present already, within you. You have a confident, positive self within you, just waiting to come to the surface. Imagine how good it will feel overcoming shyness and being filled with a feeling of confidence.

Simply relax...feeling confident...knowing you will achieve self-assurance, and the ability to interact with others and feel great. Overcoming shyness is possible. You are capable of overcoming shyness. Experience these feelings of self-assurance and calm right now.

(Pause)

Foster this feeling of confidence...and allow it to grow...enjoying how it feels to be relaxed and confident.

(Pause)

Take a few moments to hold with you a picture of self-assurance that you can recall in the future. Memorize this feeling of calm relaxation and confidence.

You can remember this feeling again in the future...any time you need to face a situation in which you experience shyness, you can recall this feeling of confidence and relaxation and experience this feeling again.

Holding this self-assurance, you can get through challenging situations. You can use this confidence in overcoming shyness.

You may even find that soon...maybe today, maybe tomorrow...you will feel motivated to face a situation that is challenging for you. Most likely, you will want to seek out other people, and talk with them...and you might even find that you feel confident, calm, not shy at all. It feels good overcoming shyness. It feels good to face situations that are challenging.

(Pause)

To conclude this relaxation session, you may want to drift off to sleep, or you might decide to reawaken and resume your usual activities.

If you choose to sleep, simply let the relaxation deepen until you drift off into pleasant sleep.

If you decide to reawaken, move your arms and legs a little, feeling your muscles waking up. Let your attention return to the present, and your mind and body return to their usual level of alertness and wakefulness.

I'll count back from three to one, and upon reaching one you will either become fully awake or drift off to sleep, keeping with you a feeling of calm and self-assurance.

Three...

Two...

One.

Guided Imagery for Writing an Exam

This guided imagery script will allow you to visualize the process of studying for and writing an exam. Visualizing success will promote increased confidence, concentration, and memory. Relaxation can also improve the ability to learn by eliminating some of the anxiety that interferes with taking in new information.

Begin reading the script here:

Begin by becoming very relaxed. Make yourself comfortable, finding a relaxed position in an environment free of distractions.

Start to relax your body, taking a deep breath in...and out.

Breathe in again...and exhale fully.

Breathe in...and out.

In...out.

Keep breathing, letting each breath relax you.

Notice some key areas in your body where tension tends to build. Your shoulders, hands, back, neck, and jaw. Focus first on your shoulders. See how your shoulders relax when your attention is focused on them. Feel the muscles loosening, and your shoulders lowering...relaxing.

Let your jaw relax, letting your lower jaw drop slightly, leaving a space between your upper and lower teeth. Feel the muscles of your face becoming smooth, loose, and relaxed.

Turn your attention to your neck. See how you can let the tension go, relaxing the muscles of your neck. Let the relaxation continue down the length of your spine, relaxing all the muscles. Feel the relaxation in your neck and back.

Now focus on your hands. Open and close your hands a few times, wiggle your fingers, and then relax. Let your hands be limp and loose, resting in your lap or at your sides.

Scan your body now for any other areas that are tense. For each one, imagine directing your breath to that area.

Imagine breathing in relaxation...and breathing out tension.

Breathing in a feeling of relaxation, and exhaling all the tension.

Feel your muscles relaxing with each breath.

Continue to scan your body, relaxing each area that feels tense.

(Pause)

Now you are feeling calm and relaxed. Your whole body feels relaxed and heavy.

Begin to visualize now the process of preparation for writing an exam. The first stage is motivation. Imagine how it would feel to be filled with motivation and drive, feeling compelled to study and write an exam.

Fully imagine this feeling, and allow yourself to experience it completely. Feel motivation.

(Pause)

You are so eager to write an exam.

Imagine now the preparation leading up to writing an exam. Picture yourself studying...interested, motivated, eager...enjoying the process of assimilating new information. You are confident and capable. See yourself studying, remembering the material, and feeling energized by this process.

See yourself studying several times, reading, writing, speaking... reviewing the information you need and committing it to memory.

(Pause)

Now see yourself in your mind's eye...you have studied and are prepared for the exam. You are feeling a bit excited to write an exam and share your knowledge...but at the same time you are feeling calm and confident about the prospects of writing an exam.

Imagine yourself during the examination. See how easy it is to recall the information you studied. Picture yourself confidently writing an exam, easily drawing upon your knowledge, answering every question, and knowing you have it right.

Some of the questions are easy, and you answer them quickly. Some questions are difficult, requiring intense thought. You were expecting this, and you are prepared.

Imagine yourself as you write an exam, taking a moment to breathe deeply, slowly, calmly...feeling your body relax and allowing your mind to become calm. In this state of calm, you are able to focus...and you answer the difficult questions thoughtfully. You experience mental clarity and concentration.

Take a few moments now to imagine the process of writing an exam, feeling calm and confident, and seeing yourself answering questions successfully.

(Pause)

Picture now that you have finished the exam. See yourself feeling confident and gratified, though you have not yet received the results. You are feeling proud of yourself for your accomplishments of studying and writing an exam. You feel calm and confident while you wait for the exam results. You may find out soon how you did, or may have to wait.

Imagine getting the exam results. Feeling confident and excited...and seeing the results: you passed! You receive an excellent grade, exactly what you were hoping for. This feeling of success and accomplishment is so wonderful, you want to write another exam just to experience it all again.

Enjoy the feelings of success.

(Pause)

Take a moment to reflect upon the process of writing an exam—motivation, preparation, writing an exam, and finding out the results. Reflect upon this process feeling calm and interested.

(Pause)

Now you have completed this visualization experience...feeling mentally prepared for the process of preparing for and writing an exam. You may even find that completing this guided imagery exercise helps you to feel motivated.

You may find that immediately after this session, you pursue one of the steps for writing an exam...perhaps you feel inclined to prepare and study...or maybe to write the exam itself.

You can anticipate success in whatever stage you are at. You are calm, confident, and in control.

Begin to wake up your mind and body...returning your awareness to the present.

Wiggle your fingers, feeling your hands and arms reawakening.

Wake up your feet and legs by wiggling your toes.

Shrug your shoulders...turn your head from side to side...feel your body waking up.

When you are feeling awake and alert, you can return to your usual activities, feeling energized, motivated, and confident.

Coping with Flashbacks Relaxation

This relaxation script is for coping with flashbacks. It can be used in the moment to help you to get through the experience and to help refocus your mind on peaceful images.

Part of this relaxation exercise will guide you to imagine that the flashbacks are like images on a TV screen, so if you want to face the fearful thoughts, you can do so. If you do not feel ready to face the images, this script includes ways of orienting yourself to the present any time you need to.

Begin reading the script here:

Start by making yourself as physically comfortable as possible. You might want to sit or lie down. It can be helpful to wrap a blanket snugly around your shoulders if you have one available. The even pressure can be calming.

The flashbacks you experience are truly frightening, but the images you have are not happening in the present. Even though flashbacks seem very real, they are only real in the past. They are not real right now.

Nothing dangerous is happening right now, even though it can feel like you are in danger.

You will get through this and you will be okay. You might not feel okay right now, but soon you will be feeling calm and relaxed.

Let's take a few moments to breathe. Breathe slowly with me now as I count.

Breathe in...2...3...4...hold...2...3...exhale...2...3...4...5...

Breathe in...2...3...4...hold...2...3...exhale...2...3...4...5...

Breathe in...2...3...4...hold...2...3...exhale...2...3...4...5...

Keep breathing slowly like this. See how calm breathing can start to center you.

During flashbacks, your attention is completely on your internal world. Relaxation can be focused on your internal world too, but on positive sensations rather than negative ones.

Focus for the next few moments on your external environment instead of your internal one. First, look around at the room you are in. Notice the details here. See the surface you are on. If you are indoors, notice the walls and ceiling around you. See the colors around you.

Now rub your hands together. Feel the friction between your palms. Feel your hands warming up a little. As your hands are warming, they are also relaxing. Now place your hands at your sides, and just notice the warmth in your hands.

Feel the surface you are on. Feel your clothes against your body. If you did choose to wrap a blanket around your shoulders, feel the comforting pressure the blanket provides.

If it is difficult to keep your attention on your environment, you can help to return your attention to the present with some physical cues. Place your hands on your knees. Now pat your knees gently, and hear the sound of your hands tapping your knees. Feel the gentle pressure with each tap.

Now rub your hands together again, focusing your attention on this sensation.

You can even place your hands on your face, and allow a gentle, firm pressure on your cheeks to calm you.

Breathe slowly, calmly...in...and out...

In...out...

Keep your breathing slow and regular.

Take a moment now to rub your hands together slowly while you breathe slowly. This calming motion can be a way to center yourself. As you continue this relaxation exercise, you can rub your hands together while breathing slowly. This can be a safe escape for you if the flashbacks get to be too much. You can take a break by rubbing your hands together and breathing slowly, any time you need to.

Now you can turn your attention to your thoughts. It's okay if you experience flashbacks. I'll be here to talk you through it. You have handled this before, and I know it is scary, but you can handle it now, too. You will get through this, and when it's over, you will feel so much better.

Maybe you are experiencing flashbacks right now, or perhaps have been throughout this exercise. Maybe you have experienced flashbacks in the past, but are not at the moment.

If you feel ready, it's okay to face those thoughts right now. If the images get too real, remember to take a break by rubbing your hands together and breathing slowly. This action will bring you back to the present, where you can remember that you will get through this and that the reality around you is neutral and safe.

I would like to take you mentally to a place of safety. Let these words guide you to a place where the flashbacks are like images on a television screen instead of part of reality. It may be frightening to watch, and at times it may seem real, but you know that the experience of flashbacks is only as real as the images on a screen.

You may have visual pictures, sounds, or physical feelings. Put them all on the screen in front of you, and you can observe them just like a movie.

This movie on the screen may be horrific, but it will be over soon. All you need to do right now is make yourself as comfortable as possible while the scary scenes pass.

If you need to look away from the screen, it's okay. You can close your eyes, or concentrate just on breathing, or do whatever else you need to do right now to cope with flashbacks.

Let's spend one minute here in front of this screen. I'll be here to talk you through it.

You are doing fine. It's okay to be scared, or uncomfortable...it's okay to feel however you are feeling.

It's okay to be frightened. It's natural to feel unsafe when you are watching something so scary.

I know this is hard. But you're getting through it. The images are not real right now, they are from the past. You are not in that place again. You are simply observing the flashback scenes on a TV screen. You know they are not real.

The minute is up. You did it.

Imagine turning the television screen off. See the flashback images and sensations disappear.

Now rub your hands together...breathe in...and out...in...and out...

Let your hands rest at your sides as you continue to breathe slowly and focus on the present. See where you really are right now.

You survived your fears. You are here, now, safe.

Look around, eyes open, observing where you are. Return to the here and now.

You may want to move around a bit to fully orient yourself to the present. Stretch your arms and legs. When you are ready, stand up, and just stand quietly for a moment, looking around.

Now take a few steps, walking around, fully present wherever you are.

When you are fully awake and alert, you can return to your usual activities, keeping with you a feeling of serenity, safety, and calm.

Relaxation for Headache Relief

Relaxation is effective in providing relief from headaches. This relaxation for headache relief script will describe ways to cope with and reduce headache pain.

Begin reading the script here:

Relaxation can allow you to influence physical responses that are usually automatic—such as blood flow and muscle tension, the primary causes of migraine headaches and tension headaches. By reversing the physical causes of headaches, it is possible to achieve headache relief through relaxation.

Before you begin, take note of how you are feeling. Notice your headache. If you were to rate the severity of this headache, with zero being no pain at all and ten being the worst imaginable pain, what rating would you assign right now? Rate your headache from zero to ten.

Find a comfortable position—sitting in a supportive chair or lying down are ideal—and start to relax your body with some gentle stretches. During this headache relief script, stop or ease up if you experience pain or discomfort. Listen to your body and make sure to stretch gently and safely.

Lower your left ear toward your left shoulder. Return to center. Lower your right ear toward your right shoulder. Return to center. Repeat, leaning left...center...right...center...left...center...right...center.

Now lower your chin toward your chest. Allow the weight of your head to stretch the back of your neck, with your muscles relaxed...no force... just allow your head to hang forward.

Keeping your head forward, roll slightly to the left and upward, back to center...now slightly to the right and upward. Your head will move left to right, tracing a slight U shape. Left...forward...right...forward...left... forward...right...forward.

Now return to a neutral position. Look up, gently leaning your head back to stretch the front of your neck. Return to neutral. Look up one more time, stretching...relaxing...and return to neutral.

Bring your shoulders up toward your ears...hold...now lower your shoulders. Bring them even lower still...Return to neutral. Repeat one more time, raising your shoulders up...and then lowering them...now relax your shoulders into a low neutral position.

Shake your shoulders front to back by bringing your left shoulder back a short distance while you move your right shoulder forward a small amount. Now move your right shoulder back and the left one forward. Repeat rapidly...shake...shake...shake. Relax your shoulders now.

Feel the tension leaving your body as you relax. Notice the beginning of headache relief as your muscles relax and let go.

Focus now on your breathing. Breathe in deeply. Feel the air you breathe in relax and sooth you. Exhale fully, breathing out all the air... relaxing as you breathe out.

Take another deep breath in...and out...in...out...

Continue breathing deeply.

Turn your attention now to your headache. Where is the rating right now, from zero to ten? Allow the headache relief to occur as you relax further.

Notice specifically where the pain is located. When you breathe in, imagine that you are breathing relaxation into this area. When you breathe out, imagine exhaling away tension. In your mind, direct your breath to this area.

Imagine now that your feet are warm, becoming even warmer. Feel the warmth increasing in your feet and in your legs.

Notice your hands, and imagine that the palms of your hands are warming. Picture your hands becoming warm and heavy...your arms also becoming warm and relaxed.

Your arms and legs are very heavy and very warm. Very relaxed. Allow the warmth in your arms and legs to increase. Warmer and warmer.

Turn your attention to your forehead. Imagine that your forehead is smooth and cool. Feel the coolness on your forehead – as if a block of ice is a few inches away from your skin, and you can feel the cool air from the ice moving gently across the skin of your forehead. Your forehead feels quite cool...you can feel that the ice is very near, but it does not touch your skin.

Allow the feeling of coolness to move along the surface of your face and head. Starting from your eyebrows, feel the cool air on your eyelids and cheeks.

Feel the coolness spreading to the top of your head, the sides of your head, the back of your head. It is so pleasant and cool. The coolness provides headache relief.

Imagine wrapping your head in a cool, wet cloth. Imagine the first strip of cloth laying across your forehead, and then above your left ear, around the back of your head, above your right ear, and over your forehead again.

Imagine wrapping your head completely in comforting, soothing coolness. It is wrapped fairly tightly, and the pressure feels good. It pushes away the pain you were experiencing, leaving only a calming firm touch. It is very cool.

Imagine that the cloth that wraps your head becomes slightly looser. Feel your body relaxing, just as the cloth is relaxing...

You can barely feel the cloth on your skin now, as it becomes looser still. You are feeling very comfortable and relaxed. Let a feeling of relaxation begin at the very top of your head. It might feel heavy...or light...it might feel tingly...feel the relaxation at the top of your head.

Allow the feeling of relaxation and to grow, expanding with each breath you take. The air you breathe in adds to the relaxation. The calm and relaxation you are experiencing allows you to experience headache relief.

The relaxation is like a bubble of peace and calm, growing larger and larger as more relaxation is added each time you breathe in. The area around the relaxation gets smaller with each breath out as you exhale any feelings of tension.

Let the relaxation grow, spreading to your eyebrows, eyelids, eyes, cheeks, nose, mouth, chin. Feel the relaxation filling up the space inside your head. Relaxing the top of your head, the back of your head, the sides of your head, your ears.

Feel the very top of your neck relaxing, and the tingly feeling of relaxation spreading down the back of your neck...the sides of your neck...the front of your neck...your shoulders.

With each breath, imagine the relaxation filling your body more and more. Growing downward from your shoulders...reaching the level of your elbows and belly button. Relaxation growing, reaching the level of your hips...knees...all the way down to your feet.

Your entire body is loose, comfortable, heavy, and relaxed.

Feel any pain or discomfort dissipating, dissolving...becoming smaller and smaller as the relaxation grows.

You can become even more deeply relaxed as you focus again on your breathing. Do not try to change anything, simply notice your breathing and focus your attention on each breath.

For the next two minutes, repeat "I am," each time you inhale, and "relaxed," each time you exhale.

I am...

Relaxed...

I am...

Relaxed...

Continue on your own for a few moments. As your thoughts wander, simply return your attention to the words you are repeating.

(Pause)

I am...

Relaxed...

I am...

Relaxed...

You are deeply relaxed. Let your thoughts drift now for a few moments as you simply enjoy the feeling of relaxation. Enjoy the feeling of headache relief. Complete and total relaxation, peace, and calm. Pleasant relief. Peaceful and relaxed.

(Pause)

You have completed the relaxation exercise. You can choose now to become alert and awake, or drift off to sleep.

I will count from five to one. If you choose to reawaken, become more alert with each number, until at one you are fully awake. If you decide to sleep, you can drift off as I count.

Five...

Four...

Three...

Two...

One.

Relaxation for Stress Caused by Work Commitments

This script is for decreasing the stress caused by work commitments. Listening to this relaxation audio right before bed can be effective to help you put thoughts of work aside so you can get to sleep, or you can listen in the moment when experiencing stress.

Begin reading the script here:

Start by making yourself comfortable, adjusting your position as needed so that you can relax. You may want to lie on your back, with your hands at your sides.

Take a few moments to focus on your breathing. Take a deep breath in...and exhale fully.

Breathe in...and out.

Slowly in...and completely out.

Keep breathing, noticing that with each breath, you can feel your body relax just a little.

Notice how your body feels right now. Scanning your body from head to feet, notice where you feel the most tense.

These tense areas are your body's way of storing worries and stress as physical tension. Concentrate on just one of these areas right now. What does the tension feel like?

Imagine that you can direct your breath to this spot. When you breathe in, imagine the breath delivering relaxation to the tense area you are focusing on. See the tension being carried away with your breath out.

Imagine each breath bringing in a bit more relaxation, and taking away a bit more tension.

Bit by bit, this area is relaxing...softening...giving up tension.

When the area you are concentrating on becomes more comfortable, move your attention to another area where your body feels tense.

Direct your breath to this area, breathing in relaxation...and breathing out tension.

Keep breathing in relaxation...and exhaling tension...for all the most tense areas in your body.

(Pause)

Notice your body as a whole...feel your body becoming more relaxed... feeling heavy...sinking into the surface where you lie.

Where is your body the most relaxed? Notice the feeling of relaxation, and allow it to grow...gradually filling your whole body with a heavy, warm, pleasant feeling of relaxation.

Feel the relaxation fill your body completely.

(Pause)

Now that you are beginning to relax, think about the work commitments that have been stressful for you. There is always work to do...always work commitments demanding your time and attention. It can feel like you are never done...one project is completed, and another comes up. You answer an email...and more emails come in. Tasks upon tasks...it seems never-ending.

Notice how you are feeling while you think about the work commitments that have been causing you stress. You may even feel some of the tension in your body coming back as you think about work.

Now let's try to put some of this stress into perspective and cope effectively. Recall the relaxed feeling you had a few moments ago. Notice that your body is relaxing, just by thinking about it. You can feel the tension draining away...becoming more relaxed with your calm, deep breathing.

The work commitments you have can be overwhelming, but think of all the things you have completed already. You have already done many tasks, that if you tackled them all at once would be impossible. You can only do one thing at a time, and by working at tasks bit by bit, you completed them.

The commitments you have right now are the same...you will get the work done, even it it's not right now. In fact, you cannot do all the tasks right now...but you can choose what to work on to finish one project at a time.

Right now, your only job is to relax. You have nothing else you need to do in this moment. Devote all of your effort and concentration to the relaxation exercise you are completing right now.

Later, when you do go to work, you can focus on one task at a time, knowing that each step you take will help you to get a project done.

You do not need to do everything at once.

You do not need to get all of your projects done right now. You will get done.

When you finish one task, you know that another will be waiting, and this is okay because you can do one thing at a time, project after project...

As a whole, your work is ongoing, but individually, projects can be completed.

Notice again how you are feeling. See that you can maintain a feeling of relaxation, and this relaxation can increase, even while you are thinking about work.

(Pause)

Now let's focus on some affirmations to shape positive attitudes for coping and to increase your resistance to stress. Repeat each affirmation in your mind after I say it, believing each affirmation to be true for you right now.

I will get my work done.

I do not need to do everything right now.

Some projects can wait, and I prioritize, choosing one at a time to work on.

I feel a sense of accomplishment when I complete a project at work.

I feel success getting one thing done at a time.

Overall my work will never be done, but I can get individual projects finished, and this feels good.

I know that there will always be more tasks waiting, and more projects to do, but I concentrate on the one task I am doing in the moment.

It is normal to feel stressed sometimes, but I can relieve this stress with relaxation.

I can let go of the things I have not yet completed. It is fine to get to them when I can.

My own expectations make me stressed. I can set reasonable expectations to be less stressed and more productive.

I decide what is most important, and do the most important task first.

I work on one thing at a time, and put aside the rest.

My time after work is time for me.

At the end of the day, my job is finished. My work commitments wait until I arrive at work the next day.

Whatever I can get finished during my regular work hours is enough.

I do not have to finish everything at once.

Now just relax for a few moments...feeling calm and relaxed.

Imagine that the work you have is like eating a cake. You cannot eat the whole cake at once, and if you try, you feel overwhelmed and sick. You take one piece of cake, and eat it bite by bite until the piece is gone. Later, you eat another piece. Eventually, you have eaten the whole cake.

Before one cake is eaten, another is already waiting. It would be impossible to eat all the cakes at once...even to eat one of the cakes at one time would be difficult and would make you sick.

Work is like a long line of cakes. It is not possible to do all the projects all at once, or to get every project done right now. By dividing your work into projects, like pieces of cake, and taking care of them bite by bite, you complete the tasks.

Taking on project after project is like eating piece after piece of cake. You cannot keep going from one thing to the next...to the next...to the next without stopping. When you eat cake, you have a piece, and then later eat another.

At work, you can complete your work hours...and then leave work for the day. The next day you will be refreshed and ready to do more work. This cannot happen if you do work in between, or think about work excessively during your time off.

You can work on projects bite by bite until completion...and at the end of the day, you no longer need to think about work. When worried thoughts come up, acknowledge them and remind yourself of the following affirmations:

There is nothing I can do right now. The work will wait until tomorrow.

When I become stressed, I can do relaxation techniques to feel calm.

My time off is time for me, not for work.

When I am not at work, there is nothing I can do about my work commitments and I do not need to worry about them.

I will get done the work I need to do.

I work on projects piece by piece, bit by bit, to get finished.

My time off helps me relax and then be more productive when I am at work.

I will get done. I don't need to get it all done right now.

Relax and allow these affirmations to be true for you right now, in this moment. Allow yourself to be free of unrealistic expectations. Relax in the certainty that you will get done the things you need to do, and that you do not need to do everything right now.

Any time you find yourself thinking about work, you can repeat the affirmations, and notice your body relaxing and your mind becoming calm.

Relaxation is productive, healing time...by taking the time to relax, you will be even more productive when you are working.

Feel a pleasant feeling of relaxation and calm...assured that you are doing what is best by relaxing right now...feeling calm and peaceful.

(Pause)

When you are ready to return to your usual activities you can choose whether to reawaken or drift off to sleep. Continue to relax for a few more moments.

In a moment, if you choose to reawaken you can open your eyes, move your muscles, and reorient yourself to your surroundings. You will become completely awake and fully alert.

In a moment, if you choose to drift off to sleep, you can gradually drift deeper into relaxation, become more and more relaxed, and fall asleep.

I'll count from ten to one. If you decide to reawaken, become more alert with each number and fully awake at one. If you choose to sleep, become sleepier and less aware with each number, drifting off to sleep at one.

Ten...

Nine...

Eight...

Seven...

Six...

Five...

Four...

Three...

Two...

One.

Relaxation for Improving One's Chess Game

Chess is a game of strategy, concentration, and planning. Relaxation can help to focus the mind to improve concentration, decision-making, and overall mental abilities. Guided imagery can also help to improve confidence. This script will guide you to relax and envision playing chess effectively to improve confidence, increase mental clarity, and improve your chess game.

Begin reading the script here:

Start by relaxing your body and mind. Begin by finding a comfortable position, seated or lying down.

Take a deep breath in, and as you exhale, allow your body to begin to relax.

Breathe slowly and naturally.

Raise your shoulders toward your ears. Then, let your shoulders relax... dropping into a comfortable, loose position, and feel yourself sinking into the surface you are on.

Allow your jaw to drop slightly, letting the muscles of your face and jaw become loose and relaxed.

Wiggle your toes once or twice and feel your feet and legs relaxing.

Gently open and close your hands once...and again...and then relax your hands and arms.

Take a deep breath in, feeling the tension in your chest and stomach as you hold that breath...and allow your chest and stomach to relax as the breath escapes slowly.

Allow the muscles of your back to relax...from your neck....to your upper back....middle back....lower back....feeling your whole body relaxing.

Notice any areas of tension in your body, and relax those areas now.

Your body will continue to relax...deeper and deeper...loose...
heavy...relaxed.

Now that you are starting to become relaxed, turn your attention
inward...and start to create a picture in your mind. See yourself playing
a game of chess. Imagine that everything is going your way. You are able
to concentrate and think clearly. You come up with the right move
every time.

You are feeling calm and confident. Fully enjoying the game of chess.
See yourself developing your pieces, planning your attack. Each move
you make is effective and brings you closer to gaining a clear advantage.

Feel a rush of energy fill your body, as you are filled with joy and
excitement playing this game you enjoy. See yourself playing chess very
well, capturing your opponent's pieces, winning the game.

At the same time as you are feeling excited and fully alive, you feel calm,
focused, and relaxed.

(Pause)

Visualize the squares on the chess board. Visualize the light squares,
then the dark squares. Now picture the whole board. Imagine that you
are playing white. Think about your king. Have confidence that you can
protect your king. Think about your favorite opening. Go through
some lines in this opening.

Maintain the feeling of calm and confidence as you imagine playing
white.

(Pause)

Now imagine you are playing black.

Think about your king as black. Think about your pawns, and your favorite defense. Have confidence that you are prepared for any opening. You are prepared to use what you know, but you are also prepared to improvise.

(Pause)

Picture yourself executing a hard-to-find combination. Imagine how you will feel...create a clear image in your mind of what this will be like.

Think about aggressive attacks and how you will stay calm although excited.

Now imagine that you've instead opted for slow, positional play. You are looking at the board. Imagine going with the flow of the game, recognizing opportunities for tactics, keeping your overall plan in mind but ready to fit it to what's happening on the board, defending effectively yet always moving forward with your plan.

Imagine what it feels like to be up material. Imagine what it feels like to have a space advantage...or to have a solid pawn structure...or to have a winning position. You are calm and serene. Think about all the different kinds of advantage you can have in a game, all the types of compensation, and see how you can turn a disadvantage into an advantage by remaining calm and making moves that use your strengths and work to lessen your weaknesses.

Whenever you experience a disadvantage, you can feel calm, assured that you can turn the disadvantage into an advantage. Fully experience a feeling of confidence, knowing that you will use your strengths.

Now imagine you are in an endgame against your opponent. Perhaps you are up material, perhaps you are equal, maybe you are even down a pawn. You already know the time on the clock. You are calm. The clock will not prevent you from making your best move. Know that your opponent is on edge about the clock, whether you are the one in time trouble or whether it is him.

Visualize gaining the advantage over your opponent with your calm and your relaxation. Your head is clear. You are focused. You are thinking about the position and what the position calls for. You know the clock calls for speed, but you will attain your speed through the clarity of the calm, through the focus of your relaxation. You are focused on the board. On your king. On your pieces if you have pieces. On your pawns.

The clock cannot make you blunder. Your calm and relaxation prevail, and you focus on the game. The clock will not make you blunder. You are relaxed, and you will not blunder. It feels good to know that you can remain so calm and focused.

Allow the clock itself to be a trigger for relaxation. The next time you think about the clock, you can associate this thought with the relaxation you are experiencing right now. A feeling of relaxation can fill your mind and body in that moment, allowing you to feel calm, focused, and relaxed during your game.

Focus your mind now in meditation to develop even deeper concentration and focus. Meditate upon the word "calm," repeating this word each time you breathe in and each time you breath out. Focus all of your attention on the word "calm."

Breathe in...calm...

Breathe out...calm...

Inhale...calm...

Exhale...calm...

Keep breathing slowly, focusing completely on the word "calm" you are repeating.

As your thoughts wander, bring your attention back to the word "calm."

Now you can simply relax, without needing to focus on anything at all. Let your mind drift...experiencing a sense of complete clarity.

See how clear your mind is now. You are able to think quickly and clearly, unimpeded by any distractions or interruptions...able to concentrate fully on the task at hand.

Relax, enjoying this feeling of mental clarity.

The next time you play chess, you will probably find that you are able to concentrate and calculate to play at a superior level. You may also experience intense mental focus accompanied by a feeling of calm.

Any time you begin to feel distracted, tense, or stuck, you can recall the feeling of relaxation you are experiencing right now, and again feel calm. The clear thinking that follows such a calm state will allow you to perform at your best.

Allow a feeling of confidence to fill your mind right now. Recall various moves, plays, and tactics that you can use in future games. Imagine the rush of joy that will accompany your success. Allow this confident, joyful feeling to grow. Fully experience pride and confidence.

Memorize this feeling you have right now...peace, calm, confidence, and relaxation. Recall this feeling often, every day taking time to experience these positive feelings.

Now it is time to reawaken your mind and body. When you are ready, start to move your muscles a little, feeling each muscle reawaken.

Wiggle your fingers and toes. Open your hands...then close them...and open them once again.

Roll your shoulders forward...and back...feeling your muscles reawakening.

Lean your left ear toward your left shoulder...return to the center...and move your right ear toward your right shoulder...then return to neutral.

Stretch a bit, feeling the energy flowing through your body.

Take a deep breath, reaching your arms up above your head as you inhale, and lowering your arms out to the sides and down as you exhale.

Take one more deep breath in, feeling fully alert and awake as you exhale. Return to your usual activities feeling calm and refreshed.

Anxiety Relief Scripts

Relaxation to Relieve Anxiety

This relaxation session will help you to relieve anxiety quickly and easily. Relaxation is a natural anxiety cure that will allow you to gain control over some of your body's automatic responses. These easy relaxation techniques can be used any time, any place, to relieve anxiety and reduce stress.

Begin reading the script here:

Some of the key symptoms of anxiety include tight, tense muscles, shallow, rapid breathing, worried thoughts, and shaking. With this anxiety relaxation script you will target each of these areas to reduce anxiety and induce the relaxation response.

First focus on breathing. Calm breathing is key to being calm and relaxed. Take a deep breath in through your nose.

Now exhale through your mouth, as if you are blowing out a candle. Blow out all the air.

As you inhale, focus on slowing down your breathing into a calm rhythm. Exhale fully, releasing all the air.

Continue to breathe slowly and calmly.

Now that you are getting the oxygen you need, realize that your only job right now is to keep yourself as comfortable as possible while this feeling passes. Fighting against the anxiety only makes it stronger, so right now, accept that you are feeling anxious. Let's focus on calming your thoughts to relieve anxiety.

Repeat the following phrases.

I am feeling anxious right now, but I am okay. This feeling will pass, and no harm will come to me. I am safe, even though I feel frightened. I will soon be calm, even though I am experiencing anxiety right now. I will get through this. I am making myself as comfortable as possible while I wait for the anxiety to decrease. I can help myself to become gradually more calm and relaxed until this feeling passes.

Continue to give yourself calming messages.

As you continue to breathe slowly in, and exhale fully, and as you continue to repeat calming thoughts, now we can address any shaking or trembling you are experiencing.

When you experience anxiety, your body is in fight-or-flight mode. Your heart is pumping quickly so that oxygen can be delivered for your muscles to allow you to use those muscles to escape from danger. There is no real danger right now, so the adrenaline is flowing through your body but not being used. Your muscles are so ready for action that they are trembling.

You can help this trembling to decrease by physically shaking out the tension. Imagine that you are shaking water off of your hands to dry them. Shake your hands. Allow your hands and wrists to be limp as you shake your hands and forearms quickly back and forth. Imagine drops of water flying off of your fingertips. Imagine your tension draining from your fingertips and being shaken away. Now stop and allow your hands to be still. Notice how much more relaxed your hands feel? They may even feel pleasantly tingly.

Continue with even breathing and calm thoughts.

Inhale, thinking, "I am becoming more and more calm."

Exhale, thinking, "I am feeling more and more relaxed."

Inhale, "calm."

Exhale, "relaxed."

The last area to focus on now to relieve anxiety is your tense muscles. Your muscles become painful, tired, and cramped as a result of stress or anxiety.

You can help your muscles relax now by first allowing your lower jaw to drop so that your teeth are not touching. Let your jaw be relaxed and loose.

Now lower your shoulders. Let your shoulders be relaxed and loose. You may even want to move your arms or shoulders in some circles, forward...and back...and now let your shoulders become limp as you increase the distance between your shoulders and your ears.

Raise your arms above your head and stretch...and now release the muscles as you gently lower your arms to your sides. Turn your head to the left, back to the center, and to the right.

Look down, look straight ahead, look up. Bring your head to a relaxed and neutral position.Straighten your back into correct posture. Keep your back upright, but maintain the natural curves of your spine.

You can continue to move, stretch, and relax to allow your muscles to become less tense.

In summary, the four steps for quick relaxation to relieve anxiety are:

1) Breathe. Remember to breathe slowly and exhale fully.

2) Calm your thoughts. Remind yourself that anxiety will pass.

3) Physically shake out the tension.

4) Relax your muscles, especially your jaw and upper back.

Continue to do these things until you feel calm and the anxiety is gone.

Relaxation for Coping with Panic

This relaxation for coping with panic script can help you to manage the symptoms experienced during a panic attack and return to a state of calm.

Begin reading the script here:

Before doing this relaxation exercise, please remember the following:

You can pause or stop this script at any time if you need or want to do so. If you find that your anxiety increases while listening to this script, here are some things you can do:

1) Wait it out. Anxiety will not last forever, and if you are able to endure the anxiety it will eventually decrease.

2) Distract yourself. Doing something else to occupy your mind and take your mind off of the anxiety can help reduce the anxious feelings.

3) Physical activity. When you experience panic or anxiety, your body is ready to fight or flee from danger. Doing something physical like walking, pushups, or jumping jacks will make use of the stress response and help the anxiety symptoms lessen.

Please remember that at any time during this script, you have the choice to wait out the anxiety, distract yourself, or do physical activity with or without continuing to listen to the script. The most important thing you can do right now is take care of yourself, and that means choosing the response that is most healthy for you at the time.

Coping with panic can take different forms, so please choose whatever method you are most comfortable with.

If you are experiencing a panic attack right now, you probably feel afraid. Even though you are terrified, you are okay. The symptoms you experience are not going to hurt you. They are a normal and natural response that will pass.

However frightening this experience is, it will not last. It cannot last. Your body will not remain in this mode because there is another normal and natural response your body is equipped with to counteract the stress response.

It is called the relaxation response. While you wait for the relaxation response to begin, you might want to do some calm breathing.

You can breathe right now. Even if it does not feel like it, you are getting enough oxygen. Your body knows how much air it needs. Notice that you are able to breathe out, right now, as if you are blowing out a candle. Take a breath in, and then imagine blowing out one small candle with a little puff of air.

Breathe in, slowly...hold that breath...and now breathe out, slowly. Let out all the air.

Breathe in...hold...and out...

Keep breathing slowly...in...and out...

Breathe in again, and then hold up one finger in front of you, as if that finger is a candle. Feel the air on your hand as you blow out forcefully through your mouth, blowing out the candle.

You can repeat this if you like. Or if you would rather, just continue your slow, gentle breathing.

Notice how your body naturally controls your breathing. You are getting just the right amount of air.

Continue to breathe naturally, deeply, slowly.

Look around you now at your surroundings. See and hear the environment around you. Notice that there is no real danger at this moment. Even though you may feel afraid right now, this fear will pass, because it is not based on anything that is here in this moment.

Look around...is there anything to fear? Is there anything you can do to make your environment feel more safe? Some people feel more comfortable if they turn a light on, or phone a friend, or read a book...even getting up and moving around a bit sometimes helps people feel more calm...what works for you?

Maybe none of those things are helpful right now, and that's okay, because the feeling of anxiety will pass. Even if you do nothing more than simply wait it out, the anxiety will decrease...get smaller and smaller...until it goes away...leaving you feeling calm.

You don't need to do anything at all right now...there is nothing you need to think about or focus on or try to do...no effort is required really at all...if you choose to, you can just sit passively...just noticing your surroundings and noticing your breathing becoming calmer and calmer...

You are okay. Even though you might not feel okay right now...you are okay.

You might want to center yourself by turning your attention now to your hands. Rub your palms together, warming your hands. Feel the friction between your two hands as you rub them together. Feel your hands warming.

See how much more grounded you feel as you notice the sensation of your hands rubbing together...you hear the swishing sound of your hands rubbing together, and you see the movement of your hands. Allow this action to help you feel centered...grounded...maybe even a bit more calm.

You can relax your hands whenever you want. Feel the feeling of relaxation as you allow your hands to just rest.

Anxiety is a normal and natural process...it is perfectly okay to feel anxious right now, although it can be terrifying. You may notice the feeling passing...you might be a bit less anxious now than you were a couple minutes ago.

Notice that the state of your mind and body is always changing. Each moment differs from the next, even if only in the smallest ways. Five seconds before this moment, you were not at the same level of tension or relaxation that you are at now. You may have been more calm or less calm, but in some minute way, you were different.

And now...you are feeling different yet...and now...and now...each moment passes by quietly, and you are more or less relaxed...always changing...

This change is a wonderful fact. It means that you cannot be as anxious moment to moment, and the anxiety cannot stay at one level. Anxiety cannot stay. Feel it slipping away, even further from your mind right now...

You are okay. The way you feel is okay.

If you want to, you can accept the way you are feeling, good or bad, right in this moment. Know that the way you feel is fleeting, changing...but accept...accept wherever you are at...

If you want to relax right now, you can allow the body's natural relaxation response to occur. This response will happen, regardless of what you do, to bring your body back to baseline...

You can rest now and just listen to the following affirmations. If you want to repeat them, please do so. You will probably find that you feel more and more relaxed and calm as you repeat or listen to these calming phrases.

Everyone feels anxious from time to time. It's okay to be anxious.

I accept the way I am feeling right now...whether anxious or calm...I accept where I am.

I know that anxiety will pass.

I feel more and more calm, moment by moment.

I am starting to feel more relaxed.

I can relax my body by breathing slowly in...and out.

I relax my muscles and allow my body to rest.

I can feel myself becoming more calm and relaxed, without any effort at all.

I accept how I feel in this moment, because it's okay to feel however I am feeling right now.

I will be okay.

I am okay.

I am feeling even more calm than I was a moment ago.

I am feeling quite relaxed.

I can choose to relax even more.

I am calm.

I am relaxed.

Peaceful.

Relaxed.

Relaxed.

Continue to relax for as long as you wish. You can continue to repeat calming affirmations until you are as relaxed as you want to be.

I'll end this script by counting to three. When I reach three, you can either continue relaxing, or return to your usual level of alertness.

One...

Two...

Three.

Generalized Anxiety Relaxation

This generalized anxiety relaxation script will help you to feel generally calmer, more relaxed, and better able to withstand stress.

Begin reading the script here:

Start by getting comfortable, finding a position seated or lying down where you can relax. Place your arms at your sides and keep your legs uncrossed to improve blood flow.

As you begin, you might want to close your eyes or focus your gaze on one spot in the room.

Take a deep breath in...filling your lungs...and now breathe out, emptying your lungs completely.

Breathe in again, through your nose...now blow the air out through your mouth.

Breathe in...and out.

In...out.

Keep breathing slowly like this, fully emptying your lungs with each breath.

Your deep breathing calms and relaxes you...allows your body to relax, to get just the right amount of oxygen, and to feel calm.

There is nothing you need to be doing right now, and nowhere you need to be, except here, relaxing, enjoying this time for yourself... enjoying this relaxation.

You deserve this time, and need this time to function at your best. This time of relaxation will allow you to be as calm and healthy as possible. Relaxation is productive, healthy time. You are looking after your health.

As you continue to breathe slowly and comfortably, turn your attention to your body. Notice how you are feeling physically. Without trying to change anything, simply become aware of the sensations in your body.

All you need to do right now is observe. However you are feeling right now is okay. None of your physical sensations are cause for concern, though some of them may be unpleasant because they are signs of built up stress.

Just notice how you are feeling, noticing any signs of stress and tension you may have without trying to change anything right now.

Scan your body, beginning at the top of your head, and moving downward. Turn your attention to your head. Observe.

Moving your attention downward, to the level of your eyes, nose, chin...down to your shoulders. Noticing each area, observing how your body feels.

Keep scanning, gradually moving down your body. How does your upper body feel? Take note of any areas of tension.

Your attention is nearing the center of your body, at the level of your stomach. How is this part of your body feeling? Keep observing your physical state. Continue to scan your body, moving the focus of your attention downwards.

Reaching the level of your hips...keep observing and moving your attention down. How does this part of your body feel? Notice any tension, without trying to change anything.

Reaching the level of your knees...how does this area of your body feel? Keep scanning...all the way down to your feet.

Take a moment now to scan your whole body, noticing how your body feels as a whole. Where is your body the most tense?

Focus intently on this one area of tension...and imagine the muscles here letting go of their hold, becoming loose, becoming relaxed...letting the tension go. Releasing the tension bit by bit, until this area relaxes.

Feel the tension softening...feel the muscles as they loosen, lengthen... warming and relaxing, as if they are melting into relaxation.

Notice where your body is the most relaxed. How does the relaxation feel? Imagine that this relaxation is warm and tingly, moving... growing...spreading to relax other parts of your body.

Feel your body becoming more relaxed as the area of relaxation grows.

Imagine that the air you are breathing is pure relaxation. Imagine that the oxygen you breathe in is relaxation, and the carbon dioxide you breathe out is tension. The air exchange is an efficient relaxation system. Feel the relaxation as you take it in through your nose and relax your body, adding to the area of relaxation already there. Expel your body's tension, breathing it out through your mouth.

Continue to exchange tension and relaxation.

Feel the relaxed area getting bigger as you breathe more and more relaxation into your body. Breathe out tension and feel the tension getting smaller.

Breathe in relaxation, and breathe out tension.

Each breath in adds to the relaxation, a full breath more of relaxation is added to your body. Each breath out removes any tension.

Keep breathing in relaxation, and breathing out tension...more and more relaxed with each breath.

(Pause)

Soon the areas of tension are very small. Your breathing can eliminate them entirely. Imagine breathing out any last bits of tension.

You are feeling so calm...so relaxed...breathing in relaxation, and breathing out tension.

Breathe in...relax...

Breathe out...relax...

Keep breathing smoothly and regularly, relaxing more and more deeply with each breath.

Now scan your body again, noticing how your body feels now.

(Pause)

Imagine that your body is made of caramel, or chocolate, or some other solid that can be melted. Right now, your body is like a solid, hard piece of caramel.

Imagine a feeling of warmth, starting in your hands and feet, that starts to soften the caramel that your body is made of.

Soon your hands and feet are soft...getting softer and more liquid. The warmth spreads throughout your body...from your hands, up your arms. Feel your arms melting, softening. It is a pleasant feeling...so relaxing.

Feel the warmth as it continues up from your feet, up your legs. Notice your legs softening, as if they are melting to a completely relaxed state.

Feel the core of your body as the warmth coming from your arms and legs meets at your stomach. Feel your core relaxing, melting.

Imagine that your whole body is very soft...like caramel that has melted and is soft and stretchy.

Simply rest, enjoying this relaxation. Floating...relaxing.

(Pause)

Focus now on your thoughts. Notice your calm thoughts. Enjoying this relaxation.

See how you can focus your thinking to a state of complete calm by meditating on a single word. Meditate now on the word, "relax," by mentally saying, "relax," each time you breathe in, and each time you breathe out.

Breathe in, "relax."

Breathe out, "relax."

Continue breathing, saying in your mind, "relax," with each breath in and again with each breath out.

(Pause)

It is normal for your thoughts to wander, and as they do, just focus again on the word "relax." Keep repeating this word as you enjoy the generalized anxiety relaxation exercise.

(Pause)

Focus all of your attention on simply repeating the word, "relax."

Keep repeating this word, noticing how you are completely relaxed and calm, drifting in a pleasant state of relaxation.

Now, simply allow your mind to drift. You don't need to focus on anything at all. Just rest, and relax, enjoying this pleasant state you are in.

(Pause)

Keep relaxing for a while longer, enjoying this pleasant, calm feeling. You can relax any time you need to take a break. This feeling of calm that you have right now can stay with you even after you are fully awake and alert.

You can keep with you the feeling of calm and confidence, and your muscles can remain relaxed. You can feel calm as you go about the activities of your life, even when you experience stress.

In fact, the next time you start to feel anxious, you might even remember this moment of relaxation and find that the anxiety goes away. You may even keep a relaxed feeling with you as you encounter stressful situations.

Imagine the confidence and composure you will have as you face stressors while still feeling calm.

Take another deep breath in, breathing in relaxation...and breathe out, emptying your lungs completely.

Keep breathing smoothly and calmly. You can breathe like this any time, drawing in relaxation, and breathing out the tension that accumulates through the day. Every day, your breathing can relax you, making you strong and resilient, able to cope with the stresses that come your way.

(Pause)

Now it is time to finish this relaxation exercise. Your energy can increase until you are fully awake, alert, and energetic.

Take a moment to wake up your body and mind so you can return to your usual activities.

Rub your hands together, feeling your hands and arms waking up.

Move your feet up and down, waking up your feet and legs.

Sit quietly for a moment with your eyes open, reorienting yourself to your surroundings.

Stretch if you want to, allowing your body to reawaken fully.

When you are fully awake and alert, you can return to your usual activities, feeling wonderful.

Anxiety Relief Meditation

This relaxation exercise uses muscle relaxation, guided imagery, and meditation to help decrease anxiety.

Begin reading the script here:

To begin, notice the places in your body that feel most tense. Anxiety can cause tension and several unpleasant physical symptoms. Relaxation can relieve these symptoms.

The very first thing to do is to breathe out, blowing the air out through your mouth, as if you are blowing out a candle.

Go ahead and breathe in when you are done exhaling.

Again, blow out all the air...and see how your lungs refill naturally.

Breathe out again...as if you are breathing out tension, blowing it away. Your lungs naturally refill, allowing you to inhale without any effort.

Breathe slowly, naturally.

Any time that your breathing feels difficult, take a moment to exhale, blowing air through your mouth forcefully to expel the tension. Continue to breathe.

Now let's relax the muscles that tend to become the most tense.

Raise your shoulders toward your ears. Then, let your shoulders relax... dropping into a comfortable, loose position...and feel yourself sinking into the surface you are on.

Allow your jaw to drop slightly, letting the muscles of your face and jaw become loose and relaxed.

Wiggle your toes once or twice and feel your feet and legs relaxing.

Gently open and close your hands once...and again...and then relax your hands and arms.

Take a deep breath in, feeling the tension in your chest and stomach as you hold that breath...

And allow your chest and stomach to relax as the breath escapes slowly.

Allow the muscles of your back to relax...from your neck...to your upper back...middle back...lower back...feeling your whole body relaxing.

Notice any areas of tension in your body, and relax those areas now.

Your body will continue to relax...deeper and deeper...loose...heavy... relaxed.

Now that your body is starting to relax, begin to create an image in your mind.

Imagine that the anxiety you experience is like a cup full of sand.

See yourself pouring the sand out of the cup...into a pile. This pile of sand is the anxiety.

Imagine blowing on the sand...and seeing some of the sand blow away. The pile is slightly smaller...a barely noticeable amount...

The next breath you exhale also blows away some of the sand.

See the pile of sand becoming ever so slightly smaller with each breath.

With each small bit of sand that blows away, you feel slightly better.

See the sand blowing away...the pile getting smaller...smaller...

(Pause)

Imagine that the pile is about half its original size...and now...how are you feeling? You might feel quite calm...relaxed...even comfortable... even though there is still some sand there.

See how this remaining sand is a manageable quantity.

What do you do with the sand now? Continue blowing it away, bit by bit? Put it back in the cup, and put it aside? Spread it out, so it is flat and smooth, instead of a pile of sand? You can choose to do with this sand whatever you wish.

You are able to change, remove, or put aside the sand. You may even imagine holding the sand in your hands, and letting it slip away through your fingers...

Imagine doing whatever it is you wish with the remaining sand.

(Pause)

Take a moment now to just relax. Rest. Experience a state of calm. Focus your attention on your breathing for a few moments, repeating the word, "relax," with each breath in...and "relax," with each breath out.

Breathe in...relax...

Breathe out...relax...

In...relax...

Out...relax...

Relax...

Relax...

Continue on your own, focusing on the word "relax."

(Pause)

Take note of how you are feeling in this moment...accepting however it is that you feel.

The sand that you imagined a few moments ago is like the anxiety you experienced. The cup in your imagination will fill up with sand again... and using your imagination, you are able to manage the sand...decrease it...

Anxiety is the same way. When it rises, you can decrease it...bit by bit... until you are comfortable...

You do not choose when the anxiety arises...but you have the ability to decrease it when it does.

Whenever you feel anxious, you can accept that you are experiencing anxiety, and then imagine pouring sand out of a cup, and blowing it away...blowing it away with each breath.

(Pause)

Keep with you a feeling of calm and relaxation as you return now to the present. Feeling calm and relaxed.

Stretch your arms above your head...feeling your muscles reawaken as you breathe in...and lower your arms, breathing out...

Move your body...feeling awareness returning to your arms and legs... the muscles reawakening...

Become more awake and alert...returning your attention to your surroundings.

When you have achieved your usual level of alertness, and are feeling awake, you can resume your regular activities, feeling calm and filled with energy.

Relaxation for Anxiety in the Stomach

This relaxation script focuses on relieving the symptoms of anxiety in the stomach. Anxiety symptoms in the belly can include nausea, butterflies, pain, tightness, digestive problems, and a general feeling of unease. This script will help to reduce anxiety and relieve these uncomfortable symptoms.

Begin reading the script here:

Begin by getting into a comfortable position. You may want to sit or lie down, with your hands resting in your lap or at your sides.

It is very uncomfortable to experience anxiety. The feeling will pass, and soon you will be feeling calm and relaxed. Trust that the discomfort you are experiencing right now is not going to last long.

Anxiety in the stomach can feel uncomfortable...even painful. Some people report a feeling of dread or unease, or feel like their stomachs are jumping.

These symptoms arise because of the fight-or-flight response. Your body is reacting with anxiety and getting ready to fight or run away...but right now, you are not in danger. You are safe, and you will soon feel better.

During this relaxation exercise, I'll describe focusing on the anxiety, and then focusing on relaxation and distracting yourself from the anxiety. You will alternate between these two areas of focus and find that the anxiety goes away.

Let's start by relaxing a little. Take a deep breath...now breathe out, emptying your lungs completely.

Breathe in slowly...and out slowly.

In...and out...

Breathe in...and out...

Keep breathing slowly like this...calm, gentle breaths.

You can relax your muscles by first tightening a muscle group, and then relaxing the muscles.

Raise your shoulders toward your ears. Then, let your shoulders relax... dropping into a comfortable, loose position, and feel yourself sinking into the surface you are on.

Allow your jaw to drop slightly, letting the muscles of your face and jaw become loose and relaxed.

Wiggle your toes once or twice and feel your feet and legs relaxing.

Gently open and close your hands once...and again...close your hands into fists...holding tension in your muscles...and then release, relaxing your hands and arms.

Take a deep breath in, feeling the tension in your chest and stomach as you hold that breath...and allow your chest and stomach to relax as the breath escapes slowly.

Allow the muscles of your back to relax...from your neck...to your upper back...middle back...lower back...feeling your whole body relaxing.

Notice any areas of tension in your body, and relax those areas now.

Your body will continue to relax...deeper and deeper...loose...heavy... relaxed.

Now that you are beginning to become more relaxed, and your muscles are letting go of tension, let's focus for a moment on the anxiety.

Concentrate your attention on your stomach, and notice in detail what the anxiety feels like. Is it painful? Does it feel like butterflies in your stomach? Maybe it is a feeling of discomfort or fear. Notice what the anxiety feels like. Think of all the words you can to describe it.

In your mind, describe the anxiety.

Well done. Now you can relax again, and think of other things. Distract yourself by noticing your breathing. Count silently with me, breathing in to the count of four, holding for a count of three, and breathing out to the count of five.

Breathe in...2...3...4...hold...2...3...exhale...2...3...4...5...

Breathe in...2...3...4...hold...2...3...exhale...2...3...4...5...

Breathe in...hold...breathe out...

Breathe in...and out...

Keep breathing slowly like this, focusing on breathing in relaxation, and breathing out tension.

Feel the tension leaving your body, bit by bit, with each breath.

Concentrate again on the feeling of anxiety in the stomach. Has it changed in any way? Describe in your mind how the anxiety feels now.

Now you can use a powerful technique to get rid of the anxiety. It seems like the opposite of what you want to do, but trust that this technique will relieve anxiety. I'll talk you through it.

Concentrate on the anxiety. Allow yourself to experience the anxiety, without fighting it...without resisting it. Just go with the anxiety. Imagine that you are floating...just relaxing, and going where the current takes you. You are safe, even though this feels scary.

See that when you do not resist the anxiety, it cannot grow. In fact, the anxiety gets weaker. This thing you were fighting, that seemed so strong, is not strong at all. You are so much stronger than the feeling of anxiety. Relax into the anxiety, allowing yourself to experience the feelings you were resisting.

(Pause)

You are doing fine. Keep relaxing into the anxiety, not fighting it...just floating. No resistance. Relaxing...

Continue to focus on the anxiety in your stomach. What I'm about to ask you to do may seem strange, but you only need to try it for a few moments. See if you can *intensify* the symptoms you experience. That's right—try to make the anxiety in the stomach get bigger. You are stronger than the anxiety, however big it may be. I'll be here to talk you though it...and you will be okay. This will not hurt you, and I'll help you relax when it's all done. Let's try it.

If you feel butterflies in your stomach, see if you can feel even more butterflies. If you feel tightness, make your stomach clench even tighter. If you feel nauseated, see if you can make the feeling of nausea grow even bigger. If you feel fear or heaviness, see if you can enlarge that feeling and make it even stronger.

Make the anxiety in your stomach bigger...as big as you can.

You may notice that nothing is happening...the anxiety isn't getting any bigger. In fact...it's getting smaller. Smaller and smaller...the harder you try to increase the feeling of anxiety in the stomach, the more it retreats from you...shrinking away.

It's like facing a monster to find out it is not a monster at all. It is a cartoon picture of a monster, and it can't hurt you. It seems funny... comical...not in any way threatening.

Feel the last bits of anxiety disappearing...and just allow it to do so. Just relax into this new feeling of mastery, this new feeling of calm. You faced the anxiety...and it did not hurt you. You went with the feeling... and it went away.

Feel a pleasant sensation in your stomach...it feels like a laugh...ready to come forward. A feeling of happiness...lightness...and joy.

You feel so free...so relaxed. You have conquered the feeling you were experiencing. Your stomach feels great.

Take a deep breath...and let it out with a sigh.

You did it.

Just relax...congratulating yourself for getting through this.

(Pause)

Whenever you feel anxiety in the future, you know now that it cannot hurt you. You know how to go with the anxious feelings, without resisting, until they pass. It's like riding a wave. You know what to do.

Take a few moments now to reawaken your body and mind, returning to your usual level of alertness and awareness.

Stretch if you want to...getting ready to return to your day.

Sit quietly with your eyes open, reorienting yourself to your surroundings.

When you feel awake and alert, you can face the hours ahead, feeling confident and calm.

Relaxation for Obsessive Thoughts

Everyone experiences obsessive thoughts sometimes, but occasionally these thoughts can increase to the point where they interfere with daily life.

This relaxation exercise will talk you through the process of dealing with these anxious thoughts and becoming more calm. This script can help with obsessive compulsive disorder and other anxiety disorders that involve worrying, obsessions, compulsions, or rumination.

Begin reading the script here:

Begin by getting comfortable, adjusting your position as needed so you can start to relax.

To begin the relaxation process, imagine that you are at the top of a stairway. At the bottom of the stairway is a state of peace, calm, and relaxation.

Take note of how you are feeling right now, at the top of the stairway.

Imagine taking a step down the stairway...a single step closer to relaxation.

Further descend the stairway, going down toward relaxation... down... down...to a state of calm and relaxation.

Picture yourself going slowly down the stairway, one step at a time. It is a comfortable, safe descent to a place of relaxation. Move down step by step, at your own pace, becoming more and more relaxed with each step you take.

Take another step down...and another...more deeply relaxed with each step.

You might even become a bit sleepy as you get closer and closer to relaxation. That's okay. Allow your mind to drift and your body to relax, heavy and comfortable.

Moving down the stairway, down, down...almost to the bottom now... when you reach the bottom you will be pleasantly relaxed.

Take the last few steps down to the bottom of the stairway...

Reaching the bottom now...a state of calm and relaxation. You are now feeling peaceful and relaxed.

Now, in this calmer state, consider the obsessive thoughts that tend to be problematic for you. People who experience obsessive compulsive disorder often feel helpless against obsessive thoughts. It can feel like the only way to get rid of the obsessive thoughts is to give in to certain behaviors, or compulsions.

You may feel compelled to avoid things, check things, count, worry, or do some other repetitive behavior. The best way to get rid of obsessive thoughts for good is to resist the compulsive behaviors and ride out the anxiety. Nothing bad is going to happen if you resist the compulsions.

Notice the obsessive thoughts right now, without taking any action to relieve this anxiety. Notice the thoughts that you are having. Focus on the thing that you are worrying about.

These thoughts will not last forever. They will go away soon, without you following through on compulsive behaviors. The urge to engage in these behaviors will pass. The anxiety will go away. Just experience this anxiety right now, without fighting it, allowing the anxiety to happen.

You are safe. Nothing bad is going to happen. You are okay, and you are riding this out.

It's perfectly okay to distract yourself. Let's try it, right now, by focusing on breathing.

Take a deep breath in...hold...and breathe out.

Breathe in...and out...

In...and out...

In...out...

Keep breathing slowly, concentrating on your breathing...focusing all of your attention on each breath you take.

(Pause)

Now focus on your muscles. Notice where there is tension in your body...and notice where your body feels relaxed.

Choose one area of tension, and allow this area to relax. Breathe in...and as you breathe out, let the muscles loosen, giving up tension.

Feel this area becoming more relaxed.

Now choose another area of tension, and relax the muscles there.

Continue to scan your body for areas of tension, relaxing each tense spot that you find.

(Pause)

Notice how you are feeling now. You are probably feeling more relaxed. See how you can relax your body, and feel more calm, without needing to act on the obsessive thoughts. Notice that by focusing on something else, such as concentrating on relaxing your muscles, you get some relief from the obsessive thoughts.

When thoughts come up, simply notice them, and then direct your attention to something else. You do not need to fight the thoughts, or try to make them go away...the thoughts will go away on their own.

All you need to do is make yourself as comfortable as you can, so that you are able to get through this stressful time. You will get through this. You are doing well.

If you start to feel too anxious, just focus on your breathing, or on relaxing your muscles, and feel the anxiety decrease.

Create a picture in your mind now, of yourself in the situation related to your obsessive thoughts. For example, if your thoughts are about contamination, imagine yourself touching a feared object. If your thoughts are about the need to check to see if the stove is off, imagine yourself getting ready to leave the house. If you have thoughts about the need to wash your hands, picture yourself standing in front of a sink. Imagine yourself in whatever situation the obsessive thoughts are about.

See yourself in this situation. What would the most healthy, effective response be? Imagine a response that does not involve compulsions... one that you would do if you did not have any obsessive thoughts. Picture yourself doing the behavior you avoid, or doing a different behavior than the one you usually do.

For example, picture yourself touching an object you are afraid to have contact with, and imagine it going just fine. See yourself leaving the house without checking the stove, and imagine yourself as you keep going, without looking back.

Create all the details of the scenario in your mind. Rehearse a new behavior in your mind...as if the obsessive thoughts have no power over you.

The obsessive thoughts do not have any power over you. You can endure the anxiety that comes up, and you will not have to endure it for long because the anxiety goes away. You only need to ride it out... waiting for the anxiety to pass...

You are stronger than the obsessive thoughts. You are much stronger... imagine yourself handling situations in a healthy, uninhibited way...free from obsessive thoughts...free from worries. Rehearse these behaviors in your mind.

(Pause)

For relief from the obsessive thoughts, you can relax your body, which we will do again in a moment. You can also practice the behaviors you have been imagining.

The best way to get rid of obsessive thoughts is to actually do new behaviors in real life. Endure the anxiety when it comes up, and it will go away without giving in to the obsessive thoughts. The anxiety and the thoughts will go away all on their own.

When obsessive thoughts become too difficult to resist, you can use relaxation to help you through it. All you need to do is to get through some anxiety temporarily...and eventually the obsessive thoughts will go away. They have no power over you now, even though this may be difficult.

You are in control. You are much stronger than the thoughts. You can resist giving into the thoughts. This will get easier and easier to do.

Focus now on relaxation. Every time the obsessive thoughts become problematic, just focus again on relaxation.

Concentrate on your hands. Feel the relaxation in your hands. Feel your hands becoming warmer, and heavier...relaxing...

Follow this relaxation as it spreads to your wrists...lower arms...and elbows.

Feel your upper arms and shoulders relaxing.

Allow the muscles of your neck...face...and head to relax.

Feel your upper back relaxing...and feel the relaxation continue all the way down your back...

Relax your sides...chest...and stomach.

Allow your hips and upper legs to relax...relax your knees....lower legs... ankles....and feet.

Allow a feeling of relaxation to fill your entire body. Let your whole body become relaxed and heavy.

Focus on your breathing...observing each breath moving in and out of your body...watching your breaths...concentrating on your breathing.

Feel yourself becoming even more deeply relaxed as you breathe...more and more relaxed.

So calm...so peaceful...completely relaxed...

(Pause)

Notice how relaxed you are feeling. Such a pleasant, calm feeling.

You were feeling anxious before, but you got through it. You have overpowered the obsessive thoughts that were bothering you. Any time you experience these thoughts again, you can relax and get through it, just like you did now.

Congratulate yourself on having gotten through this. This is proof that you are stronger than the obsessive thoughts. These thoughts have no power over you.

Now it is time to conclude your relaxation experience, while keeping with you a relaxed feeling.

Imagine that you are at the bottom of a stairway. At the top of the stairway is a state of alert and calm. With each step up, you become more and more awake.

Picture yourself beginning to ascend the stairway. Taking a step up, becoming slightly more awake, more alert.

Take another step up, and another, feeling your body and mind reawaken more and more with each step.

Continue up the stairway, nearing the middle of the stairway. Becoming more awake. More alert. Feeling your energy increasing, flowing through your body.

Climb further up the stairway...another stair...and another...more awake with each one. Nearing the top of the stairway. Only three steps left before you reach your usual level of awareness, feeling calm yet alert and energized.

Three...

Two...

One.

Guided Meditation Scripts

Beginner's Breathing Meditation

This breathing meditation script will guide you to relax by focusing on your breathing.

When learning to meditate, it is helpful to keep sessions brief so you can maintain concentration. As you become more comfortable and skilled in meditation, you can increase the duration of your meditation sessions.

Begin reading the meditation script here:

There is no right or wrong way to meditate. Whatever you experience during this breathing meditation is right for you. Don't try to make anything happen, just observe.

Begin by finding a comfortable position, but one in which you will not fall asleep. Sitting on the floor with your legs crossed is a good position to try.

Close your eyes or focus on one spot in the room.

Roll your shoulders slowly forward and then slowly back.

Lean your head from side to side, lowering your left ear toward your left shoulder, and then your right ear toward your right shoulder.

Relax your muscles.

Your body will continue to relax as you meditate.

Observe your breathing. Notice how your breath flows in and out. Make no effort to change your breathing in any way, simply notice how your body breathes. Your body knows how much air it needs.

Sit quietly, seeing in your mind's eye your breath flowing gently in and out of your body.

When your attention wanders, as it will, just focus back again on your breathing.

Notice any stray thoughts, but don't dwell on them. Simply let the thoughts pass.

See how your breath continues to flow...deeply...calmly.

Notice the stages of a complete breath...from the in breath...to the pause that follows...the exhale...and the pause before taking another breath...

See the slight breaks between each breath.

Feel the air entering through your nose...picture the breath flowing through the cavities in your sinuses and then down to your lungs...

As thoughts intrude, allow them to pass, and return your attention to your breathing.

(Pause)

See the air inside your body after you inhale, filling your body gently.

Notice how the space inside your lungs becomes smaller after you exhale and the air leaves your body.

Feel your chest and stomach gently rise and fall with each breath.

Now as you inhale, count silently...one...

As you exhale, count...one...

Wait for the next breath, and count again...one...

Exhale...one...

Inhale...one...

Exhale...one...

Continue to count each inhalation and exhalation as "one."

(Pause)

Notice now how your body feels.

See how calm and gentle your breathing is, and how relaxed your body feels.

Now it is time to gently reawaken your body and mind.

Keeping your eyes closed, notice the sounds around you. Feel the floor beneath you. Feel your clothes against your body.

Wiggle your fingers and toes. Shrug your shoulders.

Open your eyes, and remain sitting for a few moments longer. Straighten out your legs, and stretch your arms and legs gently.

Sit for a few moments more, enjoying how relaxed you feel, and experiencing your body reawaken and your mind returning to its usual level of alertness.

Slowly return to a standing position, and continue with the rest of your day, feeling reenergized.

Relaxation for Pain Relief

Relaxation of any type is effective for pain management. People who do relaxation exercises are better able to tolerate pain, and they actually feel less pain.

Begin reading the script here:

Find a comfortable position, making sure that your back is supported. Lying down or sitting in a firm chair with head support would be ideal.

As you settle into a comfortable position, just notice how you are feeling in this moment. Without trying to change anything, observe your body and mind. Pain management begins with observation.

Where is most of your tension stored?

Where is your pain located?

What part of your body is most relaxed?

Take a deep breath in...now exhale.

Breathe in...and out.

Continue to breathe slowly, smoothly.

Now continue the pain management relaxation with a passive attitude of observing. Do not try to make anything happen. Notice how your whole body feels. Passively observe, not trying to change anything. Simply take note of how your body feels.

Take a few moments now to think about the pain you experience. You may not be in pain right now. Just observe the state of your pain in this moment.

The way your body feels is always changing. The way you feel is different from moment to moment. A moment from now, you will feel slightly different from the way you feel right now. Just observe. Observe as each moment passes.

Although pain is unwanted and difficult to tolerate, try for the next few moments to regard your pain with acceptance. Accept the way you are feeling right now physically and emotionally...whether positive or negative...allow your body and mind to just be...

Accepting...observing...

You may want to repeat some pain management affirmations with me now.

I accept myself...

I accept this pain I experience...the whole of it...I accept it...letting go of the need to control or to change in this moment...

I accept the pain...

I release myself from the need to do anything right now, except just be...

I accept myself...

Now that you have repeated some affirmations, just relax for a few moments, and let go. Just be...

There is nothing you need to be doing in this moment, besides accepting this moment just as it is.

Observe again your pain...and notice that you can alter the pain slightly. See if you are able to transform the feeling, just a little...

Picture the pain...notice its exact location. Imagine that instead of pain, this area feels cool...even a bit cold...as if you have applied a comfortable ice pack to this area. Feel the coolness.

The area might even start to feel a little less cold...closer to the way the rest of your body feels...

Now focus in on this area, and imagine a slightly different feeling of your choice. You may wish to imagine the sensation of pleasant tingling...warmth...or soft but firm, comfortable pressure.

Imagine this sensation now. Imagine the sensation replacing just a tiny bit of the pain...and a tiny bit more of the pain...more and more...

Feel this new sensation growing...pleasantly...providing some relief... allowing you to relax...

Take a deep breath in...and out...

In...and out...

In...out...

Continue to breathe slowly and rhythmically as you now meditate to calm your mind.

You can choose any phrase you want to focus upon for the meditation portion of this pain management relaxation. This will be your focus word. I'll use the word "peaceful" here. Focus your attention on this word with each breath.

Every time your thoughts drift, focus in again on this word. Don't worry about making anything happen, or doing this meditation a certain way. Whatever happens is right for you at this moment.

Keep an attitude of passive acceptance. Just accept the state you are in, and continue to focus your mind on the word you will be repeating.

Breathe in...peace...

Breathe out...full...

In...peace...

Out...full...

Peace...full...

Peace...full...

Peace...full...

Peace...full...

Continue to repeat this word in your mind, focusing your attention on this word whenever your thoughts wander.

Keep repeating your focus word...

(Pause)

When your thoughts drift, focus your attention again on your focus word.

Peace...full...

Peace...full...

Focus your mind again on your focus word.

As thoughts enter your mind, as they will, just turn your attention back to your focus word.

Peace...full...

Peace...full...

Peace...full...

Peace...full...

Take note of how your body feels now. See how relaxed your muscles are. Notice how calm your mind is. Enjoy this feeling of relaxation for a few moments more...

You can keep this feeling of relaxation with you as you return to your regular activities. Complete the pain management relaxation now...memorize this peaceful, relaxed feeling, so you can return to this state whenever you need to.

Slowly reawaken your body now. Take a deep breath in...and out. Feel your mind and body becoming more awake and alert.

Move your arms and legs, and stretch your muscles to let them reawaken from this pain management relaxation.

Sit for a moment now with your eyes open, observing the room around you. When you are ready, return to your usual activities, keeping with you a sense of calm and relief.

Cue Words Relaxation

This cue words relaxation script will guide you to relax your body, and then further calm the mind by repeating cues to relax.

To begin, find a comfortable position. Become aware of how your body feels. Take a deep breath in, and as you exhale, let your body begin to relax.

Imagine that you are breathing in relaxation. Breathe out through your mouth, forcefully blowing out the air...imagine expelling tension.

Breathe in again...and exhale as if you are blowing out a candle, blowing away tension...

Breathe slowly and gently now...

Continue to take calm breaths as you focus on relaxing your body. Notice how each area of your body I mention relaxes as soon as you hear the word, "relax."

Focus on your feet...relax...

Ankles...relax...

Lower legs...relax...

Knees...relax

Upper legs...relax...

Hips...relax...

Pelvic area...relax...

Bottom...relax...

Abdomen...relax...

Lower back...relax...

Middle back...relax...

Chest...relax...

Stomach...relax...

Upper back...relax...

Shoulders...relax...

Upper arms...relax...

Elbows...relax...

Lower arms...relax...

Wrists...relax...

Hands...relax...

Neck...relax...

Face...relax

Head...relax...

Scan your body now for any remaining areas of tension. Focus your attention on these areas, relaxing them more and more.

Now that your body has started to become relaxed, I will introduce some cue words for relaxation. You can choose whatever words you like, but in this script, I will use the words, "breathe" and "relax."

With each breath in, say in your mind, "breathe."

With each breath out, mentally say, "relax."

Allow these words to relax you fully...each time you hear them, allow your body and mind to become even more relaxed and calm. Let these relaxing cue words fill your mind.

I'll guide you for a few moments, and then you can pause this script to continue repeating the cue words for another few minutes on your own.

With each breath, repeat these cue words:

Breathe in, saying in your mind: "breathe."

Exhale, saying to yourself: "relax."

Breathe...

Relax...

Breathe...

Relax...

Breathe...

Relax...

Breathe...

Relax...

Breathe...

Relax...

Breathe...

Relax...

Pause the script here to continue using these cue words on your own. After a couple of minutes, you can resume the script.

(Pause)

Continue using these relaxing cue words for a few moments longer...

Breathe

Relax...

Breathe...

Relax...

Breathe...

Relax...

Breathe...

Relax...

You are now completely relaxed...comfortable...at peace...

Observe this feeling of relaxation...memorize it...notice how calm you are...notice how your breathing is slow and regular...pleasant... peaceful...

(Pause)

Keep with you this feeling of relaxation as you become more awake and alert to return to your day.

Let your body and mind reawaken...move your arms and legs...stretch your muscles...take a deep breath in...and exhale fully...shrug your shoulders...becoming more and more awake and alert...

Let your body and mind return now to your usual level of alertness and wakefulness, feeling calm and filled with energy.

Spiritual Meditation

Meditation is effective in reducing blood pressure, decreasing anxiety, improving pain tolerance, raising mood, and counteracting the harmful effects of stress. *Spiritual* is defined here as whatever gives YOU meaning.

You may not feel any different during this session, but nevertheless, you will experience the physical and psychological benefits of meditation, especially if you engage in meditation regularly over a time.

Begin reading the script here:

During this meditation session, you will need to remain awake. The meditation process can lead to sleep, and can be used for the purpose of falling asleep, but this time the objective is to experience the relaxation response – which occurs when you are awake. Choose a position that is comfortable, but not one that will lead to sleep. You might wish to sit upright in a firm chair, stand leaning on a wall, kneel on the floor, or sit cross-legged. Find a position that is comfortable, but one that allows you to remain awake.

Get comfortable while I continue to talk for a few moments.

This script functions as a teaching or practice session of guided meditation. Once you are familiar with the meditation process, you will be able to meditate on your own, unguided. There is no right or wrong way to meditate.

The most important thing that you can do is to bring a passive attitude. *Allowing*, not forcing. *Experiencing*, not controlling. Don't worry about meditating the "right" way—just let it happen however it happens without worrying about the outcome.

It is normal to have many extraneous thoughts going through your mind throughout the process of meditation—that's okay! Just acknowledge the thoughts and bring your attention back to the phrase you will be repeating. It doesn't mean you are doing anything wrong.

When learning to meditate, you can begin with short sessions—five minutes is a good starting point—and work up to longer sessions as you become more comfortable and skilled.

Before we begin, think about your own personal spirituality. Think about what gives you meaning. You will need to select a word or a short phrase (up to about five words) that is meaningful and can be repeated within the time it takes to exhale.

For example, if religious faith is significant and meaningful for you, you might wish to repeat part of a prayer. If nature holds deep meaning for you, you might want to repeat a word or phrase relating to nature or the earth. Your meaningful phrase can relate to love, happiness, family, faith...or anything that is important to you.

You need to choose one word or one phrase and mentally repeat this phrase during meditation. For example, "peace," or, "God is love," or "Hallowed be Thy Name."

Take a moment now to choose a meaningful word or short phrase. By now you will have found a comfortable position. Small adjustments are okay, but try not to move around too much. The meditation you are about to do will be about five minutes.

Keep your meaningful phrase in mind. I'll tell you when and how to repeat it.

Let's begin.

Close your eyes or focus your gaze on one small area. Start by relaxing your muscles. When thoughts come to mind, disregard them, thinking, "Hmmm" or "oh well" and turn your attention back to your body.

Let your muscles become loose and relaxed, starting with your feet... your ankles...lower legs...knees...upper legs...pelvis...torso... back... shoulders...arms...hands...face...and head.

Feel your body...loose and relaxed...

Turn your attention now to your breathing. Notice each breath, without trying to change your breathing in any way...just observe...as thoughts arise, acknowledge them and let them go, returning your attention to your breathing...

Breathe naturally...slowly...

As your thoughts wander, simply return your attention to your breathing.

Notice your breath as it flows gently in and out of your body...without any effort...

Acknowledge your thoughts and focus again on your breathing... interruptions are normal...just let these thoughts go and return your attention to your breathing...

Now think of the meaningful word or phrase you selected...and say this word or phrase in your mind as you exhale...

Each time you breathe out, say the word or the phrase...

As your thoughts wander, bring your attention again to repeating your meaningful statement with each out breath.

Continue repeating the word or phrase each time you exhale...

Bring your attention back to the word or phrase you are repeating with each gentle breath out...

With passive acceptance, continue to focus on the word or phrase, repeating it each time you breathe out...allowing distracting thoughts to float by...

Now slowly begin to reawaken...and turn your attention to your breathing. Notice your calm, smooth breaths...in and out...allow your awareness to turn now to your body...calm and relaxed...notice how your body feels...become more aware of your surroundings...

Let your attention turn now to your thoughts...back to normal conscious awareness...normal attention to thoughts...

Sit quietly for a moment with your eyes open...enjoying the feeling of relaxation while gradually reawakening...adjust your position slightly...

Reflect upon the experience of meditation...notice what it was like... notice how you feel now...free from worries about how well you did... knowing that whatever happened was the correct and natural response.

Wiggle your fingers and toes...roll your shoulders...stretch if you like... and when you are ready, continue on with the rest of your day.

Body Image Relaxation

This body image relaxation script is a guided meditation focused on self-acceptance and self-image.

Begin reading the relaxation script here:

Take a moment to settle into a comfortable position.

Notice now how you are feeling...how you are doing right now in this moment.

How does your body feel? Scan your body for a moment now, starting at your feet, simply noticing how your body is feeling.

Notice your feet...ankles...legs...hips. Continue scanning your body, moving upward to your stomach, back, chest, sides. Mentally scan your hands, arms, and shoulders...your neck, head, and face.

Where is your body the most tense? Where is your body the most relaxed?

Just notice the state of tension and relaxation in your body.

Notice how your body relaxes...bit by bit...without any effort on your part. See how your muscles become a little bit looser...less tense... naturally, just because you are taking a moment to sit quietly and relax. Without any effort or input from you...without you even trying...your body is becoming slightly more relaxed with each passing moment.

Think about your body image...what is body image? Maybe you think about the picture in your mind you have of what your body looks like. Maybe it's the ideas you have about your body...your feelings about your physical self. Perhaps body image is a vision of how you think your body should be. What does body image mean to you?

Take a moment now to consider your thoughts and ideas about your own body. How are you feeling right now, thinking about your body image? You might feel neutral, content, comfortable, uncomfortable,

satisfied, dissatisfied, happy or unhappy, angry, afraid, accepting...
maybe a combination of things...contradictory feelings are common...
and it is okay to feel however you are feeling.

What might it be like to accept your body, just as it is? What if you felt
okay about your physical self? Imagine for a few moments what that
would be like.

Think about a time in your life when you felt accepting of your physical
self—your whole self, or even part of yourself.

Which parts of your body are the easiest for you to accept?

Imagine if you could accept your body as a whole, rather than as a
collection of individual parts.

You have been doing some difficult thinking these last few moments.
Let's take a step back now, mentally, to relax.

Breathe in, deeply...and breathe out.

In...and out...

In...and out...

Keep breathing deeply, slowly. It feels good to take deep, calm breaths.

Just relax for a moment while you notice your breathing. Just notice
your breaths for a moment.

(Pause)

If there are any areas where you are feeling tense, direct your attention
to these areas as you breathe...imagining that each breath in brings
relaxation...and each breath out expels tension.

Breathing in relaxation...and breathing out tension...each breath relaxes you further.

(Pause)

Now I will say some body image affirmations. You can repeat these if you wish, or simply relax as I talk.

Each affirmation is true...even if it may not seem true right now.

Let's begin the affirmations.

I am okay the way I am.

I can accept myself the way I am.

My body is acceptable just the way it is.

I am an okay person.

I accept this body I am in.

There is no need to be perfect.

My imperfections make me unique.

I am perfectly alright just the way I am.

My body is a functioning whole.

I am human, and all humans have flaws.

I can accept my imperfections.

I free myself from judging my body.

I am okay just the way I am.

I accept myself.

Now that you have repeated some affirmations, take note of how you are feeling. What was it like to repeat or listen to the affirmations?

It is okay to feel however you are feeling right now, good or bad. Accept the variety of feelings you may have.

Take a moment now just to relax. Let all the worries and tension go as you breathe slowly in...and out...in...out...continue to breathe slowly, deeply...naturally.

When you are ready to return to your waking level of consciousness, slowly leave this relaxed state you are in. Keep with you a feeling of calm, while becoming more awake and alert.

Wake up your body and your mind. Move your arms and legs a little and feel your muscles reawakening.

I'll count up now from five to one, and when I reach one you will be fully awake and ready to return to your usual activities.

Five...

Four...

Three...

Two...

One.

Counting Meditation

This counting meditation script will guide you to relax with meditation using counting. Counting will allow you to focus your mind, which will lead to deep relaxation.

During this meditation, it is normal for your mind to wander. When you notice your attention drifting, simply focus again on your breathing. Try to passively accept thoughts that enter your mind, and allow them to pass without paying particular attention to them.

To begin, find a comfortable position, such as sitting in a firm chair, or cross-legged on the floor. Take a moment to notice how your body feels. Observe, without trying to change anything.

Notice any areas of tension...and notice which parts of your body feel relaxed.

Sit quietly, and turn your attention to your breathing.

Breathe slowly, deeply...in...and out...

In...out...

As you continue to breathe, count each breath out.

In...one...

In...two...

In...three...

In...four...

In...five...

Keep counting on your own now...focusing all your attention on your breathing...and on the numbers...

(Pause)

As your attention drifts, focus again on your breathing...

(Pause)

If you lose count, simply start again at one.

(Pause)

Keep focusing on your breathing...and continue counting each exhalation.

(Pause)

Don't worry if your attention wanders; just return your focus to your breathing.

(Pause)

Now you can stop counting and simply relax for a few moments. Just be.

(Pause)

Enjoy the feeling of relaxation. Notice how you are feeling now, physically and mentally, and notice how it feels to be more relaxed.

(Pause)

When you are ready to conclude your meditation session, take a few moments to reawaken your mind and body.

Turn your attention to your surroundings. Notice the sights and sounds around you as you become more aware and alert.

Move your arms and legs, feeling your body reawaken. Stretch if you want to. Feel your body waking up.

When you have returned to your usual level of wakefulness, you can return to your usual activities, keeping with you a feeling of calm.

Learn an Instrument Meditation

Feeling relaxed and confident can help you learn an instrument or other new skill more easily. This meditation aims to help increase confidence and motivation when learning to play an instrument.

Begin reading the script here:

Find a comfortable position in an environment free of distractions. Loosen any tight clothing, and adjust your position until you are comfortable.

To begin the relaxation process, imagine that you are at the top of a stairway. At the bottom of the stairway is a state of peace, calm, and relaxation.

Take note of how you are feeling right now at the top of the stairway.

Take a deep breath in...and out.

Breathe in...and out.

Take another deep breath...and relax as you exhale.

Keep breathing slowly and deeply, remembering to exhale fully between each breath.

Imagine taking a step down the stairway...a single step closer to relaxation.

Further descend the stairway, going down toward relaxation...down... down...to a state of calm and relaxation.

Picture yourself going slowly down the stairway, one step at a time. It is a comfortable, safe descent to a place of relaxation. Move down step by step, at your own pace, becoming more and more relaxed with each step you take.

Take another step down...and another...more deeply relaxed with each step. Feel your arms becoming very heavy...so heavy you can hardly lift them...it is a good feeling of relaxed heaviness. Allow your arms to rest at your sides...feeling loose and heavy. Your legs might even be getting heavier as well. Feel the heaviness in your legs...a warm, pleasant feeling.

You might even become a bit sleepy as you get closer and closer to relaxation. That's okay. Allow your mind to drift and your body to relax, heavy and comfortable.

Moving down the stairway, down, down...almost to the bottom now... when you reach the bottom you will be pleasantly relaxed. Notice how your whole body is relaxed and heavy now. Becoming more and more relaxed...deeper and deeper.

Take the last few steps down to the bottom of the stairway...

Reaching the bottom now...a state of calm and relaxation. Peaceful and relaxed.

Rest quietly for a few moments...enjoying the relaxation you are experiencing.

(Pause)

Think now about a skill you would like to learn. Perhaps you want to learn an instrument...learn to play the guitar for example. Notice how being relaxed allows you to think with clarity, and prepares you for optimal learning.

You are fully capable of learning this new skill. Imagine yourself learning, practicing...easily picking up the skills you desire...easily memorizing and remembering the necessary details.

Picture yourself as you learn an instrument...learning to play skillfully, and enjoying the process. See yourself as you play for fun...and as you enjoy yourself, you are picking up a new skill.

Imagine yourself playing the notes easily and accurately.

You may notice that you are filled with a desire to learn an instrument, full of motivation and interest in playing and learning.

You might even find yourself practicing for a few minutes each day to learn an instrument.

Notice that you can review mentally the process of playing the instrument. This mental practice is as effective as physically practicing.

Take a moment now to envision yourself practicing, learning this new skill that is important to you.

(Pause)

This meditation to learn an instrument is most effective when followed by actual physical practice. Perhaps you will find a few minutes after this session concludes to actually pick up the instrument and practice.

Feel the excitement and interest...looking forward to the enjoyment you will experience with playing the instrument. Learning is enjoyable. Know that you will make mistakes as you go, and will learn from them to become even more skilled.

Take a few moments now to enjoy how relaxed you are feeling...and to enjoy the anticipation of looking forward to practicing...eager to learn an instrument.

Feel your confidence building, knowing that you can quickly and easily expand your skills.

Enjoy the confidence, the anticipation, the interest you feel. Learning new skills enhances your life. You are probably looking forward to the richness this new skill...this hobby...will bring.

(Pause)

Take a few more moments to meditate on the idea of learning to play an instrument...feeling a range of positive emotions as you think about the process.

Now it is time to conclude your relaxation experience, while keeping with you a relaxed feeling.

Imagine that you are at the bottom of a stairway. At the top of the stairway is a state of alert and calm. With each step up, you become more and more awake.

Picture yourself beginning to ascend the stairway. Taking a step up, becoming slightly more awake, more alert.

Take another step up, and another, feeling your body and mind reawaken more and more with each step.

Continue up the stairway, nearing the middle of the stairway... becoming more awake....more alert...feel your energy increasing, flowing through your body.

Climb further up the stairway, another stair, and another, more awake with each one...nearing the top of the stairway. Only three steps left before you reach your usual level of awareness, feeling calm yet alert and energized.

Three...

Two...

One.

Affirmations for Self-Esteem

This affirmations for self-esteem relaxation script includes affirmations to increase self-esteem and confidence and promote a general feeling of calm.

Begin reading the script here:

Begin to relax, finding a comfortable position and starting to let the tension leave your body.

Imagine that you are at the top of a stairway. At the bottom of the stairway is a state of peace, calm, and relaxation.

Take note of how you are feeling right now, at the top of the stairway.

Imagine taking a step down the stairway...a single step closer to relaxation. As you take this step, feel your arms relaxing...becoming heavy.

Limp...loose...relaxed.

Further descend the stairway, going down toward relaxation...down... down...to a state of calm and relaxation. Feel your legs relaxing and becoming limp. Your legs are feeling very heavy...so heavy...feel your legs sinking down, the heaviness pulling your legs down into relaxation.

Picture yourself going slowly down the stairway, one step at a time. It is a comfortable, safe descent to a place of relaxation. Move down step by step, at your own pace, becoming more and more relaxed with each step you take.

Feel the heaviness in your arms and legs...your arms are so warm and so heavy...feel gravity pull on your arms gently, pulling your shoulders down into a relaxed position.

Take another step down...and another...more deeply relaxed with each step. Feel your neck and back relaxing...feeling warm, loose...relaxed.

You might even become a bit sleepy as you get closer and closer to relaxation. That's okay.

Allow your mind to drift and your body to relax, heavy and comfortable. Your head and face relax.

Feel the muscles of your face becoming limp, soft, relaxed. Your eyelids are very heavy. It feels so good to close your eyes...your eyelids are so heavy, you cannot keep them open. So heavy and relaxed.

Moving down the stairway, down, down...almost to the bottom now... when you reach the bottom you will be pleasantly relaxed.

The closer you get to the bottom, the heavier and more relaxed you feel. Your body is so heavy...but at the same time feels light, as if floating. It is an unusual feeling, but pleasant. So peaceful. Drifting in calm relaxation.

Take the last few steps down to the bottom of the stairway...sinking into relaxation. So heavy and relaxed.

Reaching the bottom now...a state of calm and relaxation. You are now feeling peaceful and relaxed.

Now I'll repeat some affirmations for self-esteem. You don't even have to listen or pay attention, you can simply relax while I talk.

Just let your mind drift, and reflect upon these affirmations in the back of your mind, with your subconscious. You can take in the affirmations if you choose to and if they are a good fit for you, and disregard any that do not apply.

Just relax now and let your mind drift for the remainder of this relaxation exercise.

At the end of the script, I'll count back from five to one, and you can choose to reawaken or drift off to sleep...but for now, just relax...letting your mind drift...there is nothing you need to do...nothing you need to focus on...just relaxed and calm.

Just let these words drift in your mind, without needing to focus especially on any of them.

You are a worthwhile person.

You are capable of achieving many things.

You deserve to be happy. You can be happy even through difficult circumstances.

You can handle the problems that come your way.

You are a strong person...while understanding that no one needs to be strong all the time.

You are okay...a good person.

Your worth is not measured by achievements, appearance, or other external things. You are worthwhile as a person, just the way you are.

You are perfectly alright, just the way you are.

Accept yourself.

Be kind to yourself.

Take good care of yourself physically and emotionally.

You are okay the way you are.

(Pause)

Continue to allow your mind to drift, as you just relax. Allow these affirmations to be true for you, repeating them silently in your mind if you want to, or simply taking them in.

I am a worthwhile person.

I deserve to be happy. I deserve good things.

I am a human being with flaws. It is okay to have flaws.

I am unique, and I appreciate my uniqueness.

I am perfectly alright, just the way I am.

I feel good about myself.

It is okay to like myself.

I am likable.

I have many good qualities.

I am a decent human being.

I do some things wrong and many things right.

I learn from my mistakes, and forgive myself when I make them.

I take time for myself. I deserve this time, and need this time.

I take care of others and I take care of me.

I accept help, support, and love from others.

I am confident.

I hold myself in high regard.

I like myself.

I accept myself.

I am not perfect, and that is okay.

I accept myself.

(Pause)

Continue allowing your mind to drift...relaxing. Let the affirmations for self-esteem become true for you, filling you with a sense of confidence and self-assurance.

You are capable of making positive changes...capable of increasing your self-esteem...and of nurturing your self-esteem.

Simply relax now, noticing what it is like to feel good about yourself... allowing yourself to feel calm and confident.

(Pause)

Keep with you this feeling of self-esteem. Remember the affirmations for self-esteem, taking them in and believing them as truth for you.

You can continue to feel good about yourself and keep this feeling of self-assurance, even after you have finished this affirmations for self-esteem script.

I'll count now from five to one, and you can choose to drift off to sleep or become fully awake. When I reach one, you will be either in a state of deep sleep or you will be fully alert and awake, depending on how you have chosen to conclude this affirmations for self-esteem script.

Five...

Four...

Three...

Two...

One.

Learn a Language Meditation

This meditation script will help with learning a language by guiding you to relax and by helping to improve your concentration.

Start by getting comfortable and setting aside a few minutes when you can relax undisturbed.

Choose a position seated or lying down, and start to relax your body. Sit quietly, noticing how your body feels.

Find one area in your body that is the most tense. Focus on this area, observing the tension there. As you breathe, imagine that you are breathing in relaxation, and breathing out tension. Direct the breath to the area of tension, directing relaxation into this area, and breathing tension out of the area.

Breathe in relaxation...and breathe out tension.

Breathe in relaxation...and breathe out tension.

Keep breathing, feeling this area you are focusing on relaxing more and more with each breath.

Scan your body now for further areas of tension. For each spot of tension that you find, direct your breathing to that area, imagining that relaxation is drawn into the area, and breathing tension out.

(Pause)

Turn your attention inward now...inside your imagination. Now that you are starting to relax, you can use this time to calm your mind in preparation for learning a language. As you relax, mental clarity increases. Memory improves. Notice your concentration and attention increasing. Your abilities are optimal for learning.

Imagine feeling calm and confident, eager to learn. Feel the joy you experience at succeeding in learning a language.

Allow words and phrases to flow through your mind...the familiar elements of this language you are mastering. Learning a language feels so easy...so natural. You feel competent, skilled, relaxed.

Learning a language is fun and enjoyable. Imagine yourself learning eagerly, remembering easily, confidently learning and speaking the language you have chosen.

The words are like music...you love to hear them, listen to them... remember them.

Imagine learning a language, mastering a new language, hearing and feeling the language flowing. Committing words, phrases, ideas to memory. Calmly and comfortably speaking, understanding.

(Pause)

Take a few moments now to meditate upon the language you are learning. You might want to choose a phrase in your language of choice...something brief but meaningful that you can repeat.

Choose a phrase, and repeat it silently in your mind. Each time you breathe in, repeat your phrase. Each time you breathe out, repeat the phrase. Allow all other thoughts to simply pass through your mind, without dwelling upon them.

(Pause)

Every time your thoughts wander, simply return to focusing on the phrase you have chosen.

(Pause)

It is normal for thoughts to wander...just focus again on the phrase you are repeating.

(Pause)

Feeling deeply relaxed, calm, and confident.

Keep repeating your chosen phrase.

(Pause)

Now you can just sit quietly for a moment, letting your thoughts drift, allowing your mind to wander. Enjoy the relaxation and mental clarity you are experiencing.

(Pause)

Imagine yourself when you have finished this meditation. Imagine being filled with a feeling of eagerness, excitement...ready to learn. See yourself doing something to practice the language you are learning, or doing an activity to help with learning a language.

Perhaps you will listen to the spoken language...or take a few minutes to practice speaking it yourself. Maybe you will do some homework or courses related to learning a language. Picture something you can do right after you finish this meditation, something that will bring you closer to mastery of this new language.

(Pause)

When you are ready to finish this meditation, give yourself a few moments to reawaken your mind and body.

Take a deep breath in, and feel your body reawaken as you exhale.

As you inhale, reach up, stretching your arms, and return your arms to your sides as you exhale.

Keep breathing, awakening more and more with each breath.

Sit for a moment with your eyes open, reorienting yourself to your surroundings.

When you have returned to your usual level of alertness and are fully awake, you can return to your day, feeling calm, clear, and relaxed.

Relaxation to Deal with Anger

This guided relaxation script describes how to deal with anger quickly and effectively in the moment. It guides you in controlling anger in a healthy, productive way.

Begin reading the script here:

It's time to take a break...and relax...to deal with anger in a healthy, productive way.

Anger is a normal and natural emotion, and there is nothing wrong with having feelings—you are human, after all. You have the power to decide how to deal with this emotion you are experiencing.

Anger management does not mean holding anger in. It does not mean that you will never feel angry. Anger management is managing the behavioral responses that can arise when you are feeling angry.

All you really need to do right now is take a few moments just to relax, for you, to help you feel relaxed and calm. It feels good to relax.

After this short relaxation session is over, you can proceed with your day, and react in a way that you choose...relaxing for a moment now will help you to react calmly, rather than acting out of emotion.

It's okay to be angry. Just allow yourself to feel however it is you are feeling right now, noticing this feeling, but not reacting just yet. All you're doing is observing. Emotions are neither right nor wrong...they just are.

Take a deep breath in. Hold for a moment, and now breathe out.

Breathe in...hold that tension...and now breathe out...feeling the tension release with your breath.

Breathe in...and out...

In...out...

Keep breathing like this, slowly...deeply...and let your body relax a little.

Turn your attention again to how you are feeling. Notice the physical sensation of anger. Where in your body is the anger stored? Some people notice that they tighten their shoulders when they are feeling angry. Others who deal with anger notice clenched fists or a tight jaw. Anger may be experienced as a feeling in the stomach...the neck...any one of a number of places in the body demonstrate physical symptoms of anger.

Many of these physical symptoms are uncomfortable. Some of these symptoms can be relieved right now, if you like, by relaxing your muscles. Let's relax a few areas to begin this process to deal with anger by relaxing your muscles.

Starting with your hands and arms, first tighten your hands into fists. Feel the tension in your hands and arms. Hold...tighter...tighter...and relax. Let go, allowing your hands and arms to be relaxed, loose, and limp. Notice the difference between tension and relaxation.

Now see if you can create a feeling of relaxation in your shoulders. Take a moment to relax your shoulders now. You may choose to tighten the muscles, and then relax, or you can simply relax your shoulders without tensing them first. Do whatever seems to work the best.

Focus now on your face and jaw. Relax your face and jaw, tensing first if you want to. Let all the tension leave your face...let the tension leave your jaw...leaving your face and jaw limp, smooth, and relaxed.

Scan your body now for remaining areas of tension. Relax each area that feels tense...scan your body from head to toe...relaxing each part of your body.

(Pause)

Take note of how you are feeling now. Physically. Emotionally.

You are controlling anger right now, just by the fact that you have not yet reacted with angry behaviors. You have chosen to relax, to deal with anger in a healthy way.

To increase the control you have over anger, you may want to repeat some affirmations to help create realistic, rational thinking...also called self-control thoughts.

Here are five affirmations for anger management to help deal with anger:

I acknowledge that I am feeling angry right now, and accept the way I feel.

I have the power to control my reactions.

I can fully experience this anger, yet wait before I take action.

I can feel angry, but calm and in control at the same time.

It's okay to feel angry.

Notice again how you are feeling. Physically, how are you feeling? Let your body relax a little more...relaxing any tense areas.

Emotionally, how are you feeling? See how emotions come and go... anger can come and go...it will not last forever. There is a limited time when you exercise self-control, before the anger is no longer an issue.

You may feel less angry...just as angry...or more angry now than you were at the beginning of this relaxation session.

To deal with anger that may remain, you may need a way to express the anger and get it out. You do not have to keep your emotions inside... you can choose how to express them.

You can let anger out by breathing deeply...breathing in relaxation, and breathing out anger...letting anger go with each breath.

There are other ways to express anger, too. You can do any of these activities after this script to allow yourself freedom to express the anger you experienced. Physical exercise, journaling, talking to someone you trust...there are many ways to express yourself.

After the anger has decreased and you are feeling calm, you might want to address the situation that was upsetting by taking action to change the situation, or by speaking to the person you were upset with. Or you may just choose to let the situation go.

Once your anger has decreased you can choose whatever option seems best. You have the right to feel a range of emotions, including anger, and to express these emotions in healthy ways that you choose.

I'll conclude this script with some breathing.

Take a deep breath in...and out...

In...out...relaxing with each breath

In...out...

In...out...

Keep breathing deeply to deal with anger and feel relaxed and calm.

Congratulate yourself for dealing with anger through relaxation.

I'll count now from five to one. Imagine that right now, you are at a five, and that when I reach one you will be feeling awake and alert, yet calm, peaceful, and relaxed.

Five...

Four...

Three...

Two...

One.

Physical Relaxation Scripts

Passive Progressive Relaxation

This passive progressive muscle relaxation guides you to relax each part of your body from head to feet.

Begin reading the relaxation script here:

Find a comfortable position. Lie on your back or sit in a chair with your back supported.

Place your hands at your sides, palms up.

Close your eyes if you wish.

Now begin to become aware of your breathing...focus on slowing down the rhythm of your breathing...your chest and abdomen will expand outward with each breath, like a balloon gently filling with air...

Imagine your ribcage moving out to the sides when you inhale...and gently inward as you exhale...

Slowly take a deep breath in...pause for a moment...and then exhale slowly. Let the tension melt away as you relax more deeply with each breath...

Continue breathing slowly and gently...

Now turn your attention to the top of your head. Feel the relaxation beginning at the top of your scalp and spreading slowly downwards...

Even your ears are becoming relaxed and heavy...feel your eyebrows resting, gently resting downward...your forehead is becoming relaxed and smooth...

Allow your temples to relax...let your jaw relax by allowing your mouth to be slightly open with your lips apart, or gently touching...allow your tongue to relax...

Feel your throat relaxing...relax your cheeks, nose, and eyes...feel your eyelids becoming very heavy...and very relaxed...more and more relaxed...

Continue to relax...enjoy the feeling of relaxation you are experiencing.

Now turn your attention to your neck...allow a feeling of relaxation to begin at the top of your neck and flow downward...

Feel the relaxation as your shoulders become relaxed and loose...let your shoulders gently sink downward...as they become relaxed...and heavy... very heavy...and very relaxed...deeper and deeper...relaxed...

Feel your collar bones becoming relaxed as your shoulders move gently back, and your chest widens slightly...

Allow all the muscles in your shoulders to feel smooth...and relaxed...as the muscles give up their hold completely...

Continue the passive progressive relaxation...enjoy the feeling of relaxation you are experiencing.

Notice your breathing once again...see how regular it has become... continue to take slow...smooth...deep breaths...breathe in the feeling of relaxation...and breathe out any tension...your breathing allows you to become more and more relaxed...deeply relaxed...

Now turn your attention to your right arm...feel the relaxation flowing down from your right shoulder...allow your upper arm to relax...your elbow...lower arm...and wrist become loose and relaxed...

Enjoy the feeling of relaxation as the muscles of your right arm give up their hold...feel the relaxation flowing into your hand...let all the tension drain out each fingertip and flow away...the relaxation spreads to your thumb...index finger...middle finger...ring finger...and little finger...

Feel the relaxation flowing down your left arm...let the muscles of the left upper arm relax...relax your elbow...lower arm...and wrist...feel the relaxation flowing down your left arm...

Let the tension melt away...imagine the tension flowing right out your fingertips...allow your left hand to relax completely...relax your thumb... index finger...middle finger...ring finger...and little finger...

Both of your arms are now totally relaxed...allow them to be free and limp...pleasantly relaxed...

Enjoy the feeling of relaxation you are experiencing...let the relaxation continue to flow...spreading easily down your body...continue to relax...

Allow the feeling of relaxation to continue to your chest and stomach... feel the relaxation there...becoming deeper with each breath...

Now turn your attention to your upper back...feel the relaxation flow down your spine...let all the muscles give up their hold...relax your upper back...middle and lower back...allow your back to relax completely...feel the relaxation in your whole upper body...

Relax more deeply with each breath...more and more relaxed...deeply relaxed and calm...

Let your hip muscles relax...relax all the way from your buttocks, down the back of your thighs...relax the muscles on the front of your thighs...

Feel the relaxation in your upper legs moving down to your knees...your calves and shins...your ankles...and your feet...allow all the muscles to relax and go limp...

Allow any last bits of tension to flow right out the soles of your feet... feel the relaxation flowing through your body...from the top of your head...down to the bottoms of your feet...become more relaxed with each breath...enjoy the feeling of total relaxation...

You are now as relaxed as you want to be...experience the feeling of deep relaxation...enjoy the feeling...relaxed...calm...at peace...

Focus on the feeling of relaxation throughout your body...notice your breathing...your relaxed muscles...your calm thoughts...memorize this feeling so you can re-create this relaxed state whenever you wish...

Enjoy relaxing for a few moments more...

When you are ready to return to your day, reawaken your body slowly... gently move your muscles...roll your shoulders slowly forward... then slowly backward...lean your head gently to the left...return to the center...lean your head gently to the right...return to the center...turn your head...

Wiggle your fingers and toes...

Gently open your eyes...feeling alert...calm...and full of energy.

Progressive Muscle Relaxation Exercise

Progressive muscle relaxation exercises are relaxation techniques that involve progressively tensing and then relaxing muscles or muscle groups.

By tightening a muscle and then releasing, you can feel the difference between tense and relaxed. Actively engaging in progressive muscle relaxation exercises effectively loosens and relaxes the muscles.

Sometimes if you are very tense already, actively tensing your muscles will not be helpful. If this is the case, you may want to try passive progressive muscle relaxation exercises instead.

Begin reading the relaxation script here:

Make sure not to do any movements that cause pain. If any of these exercises causes discomfort, ease up or stop to ensure that you do not cause muscle cramping or injury.

Begin by finding a comfortable position sitting, standing, or lying down. You can change positions any time to make yourself more comfortable as needed.

The first progressive muscle relaxation exercise is breathing. Breathe in forcefully and deeply, and hold this breath. Hold it...hold it...and now release. Let all the air go out slowly, and release all the tension.

Take another deep breath in. Hold it...and then exhale slowly, allowing the tension to leave your body with the air.

Now breathe even more slowly and gently...breathe in...hold...out...

Breathe in...hold...out...

Continue to breathe slowly and gently. Allow your breathing to relax you.

The next progressive muscle relaxation exercise focuses on relaxing the muscles of your body.

Start with the large muscles of your legs. Tighten all the muscles of your legs. Tense the muscles further. Hold onto this tension. Feel how tight and tensed the muscles in your legs are right now. Squeeze the muscles harder, tighter...continue to hold this tension. Feel the muscles wanting to give up this tension. Hold it for a few moments more...and now relax. Let all the tension go.

Feel the muscles in your legs going limp, loose, and relaxed. Notice how relaxed the muscles feel now. Feel the difference between tension and relaxation. Enjoy the pleasant feeling of relaxation in your legs.

Now focus on the muscles in your arms. Tighten your shoulders, upper arms, lower arms, and hands. Squeeze your hands into tight fists. Tense the muscles in your arms and hands as tightly as you can. Squeeze harder...harder...hold the tension in your arms, shoulders, and hands. Feel the tension in these muscles. Hold it for a few moments more...and now release. Let the muscles of your shoulders, arms, and hands relax and go limp.

Feel the relaxation as your shoulders lower into a comfortable position and your hands relax at your sides. Allow the muscles in your arms to relax completely.

Focus again on your breathing. Slow, even, regular breaths. Breathe in relaxation...and breathe out tension...in relaxation...and out tension... continue to breathe slowly and rhythmically.

Now focus on the muscles of your buttocks. Tighten these muscles as much as you can. Hold this tension...and then release. Relax your muscles.

Tighten the muscles of your back now. Feel your back tightening, pulling your shoulders back and tensing the muscles along your spine. Arch your back slightly as you tighten these muscles. Hold...and relax. Let all the tension go. Feel your back comfortably relaxing into a good and healthy posture.

Turn your attention now to the muscles of your chest and stomach. Tighten and tense these muscles. Tighten them further...hold this tension...and release. Relax the muscles of your trunk.

Finally, tighten the muscles of your face. Scrunch your eyes shut tightly, wrinkle your nose, and tighten your cheeks and chin. Hold this tension in your face...and relax. Release all the tension. Feel how relaxed your face is.

Notice all the muscles in your body...notice how relaxed your muscles feel. Allow any last bits of tension to drain away.

Enjoy the relaxation you are experiencing. Notice your calm breathing... your relaxed muscles...Enjoy the relaxation for a few moments...

When you are ready to return to your usual level of alertness and awareness, slowly begin to reawaken your body. Wiggle your toes and fingers. Swing your arms gently. Shrug your shoulders. Stretch if you like.

You may now end this progressive muscle relaxation exercise feeling calm and refreshed.

Stretch and Relax

This stretch and relax script will guide you to relax your body by stretching out key areas to decrease the tension in your muscles.

Begin reading the relaxation script here:

In this stretch and relax script, we will begin with the most important key areas to release tension, and then proceed to stretch muscle groups from the feet upward. Take a deep breath in...hold...and breathe out... releasing tension. Continue to breathe rhythmically throughout these exercises.

None of these exercises should cause pain. If you experience any discomfort, stop or ease up. All of these stretches should be done gently and comfortably. Stretch until you feel a slight pull, not until you feel pain.

The first key area to stretch and relax is the neck and shoulders.

Turn your head to the right, gently looking over your right shoulder...

Breathe in...and out...

Now return to the center.

Turn your head to the left...breathe in as you look over your left shoulder...and out as you return to the center.

Turn again to the right...now back to the center...and turn to the left...and back to center.

Take a deep breath in.

Facing straight ahead, exhale as you look down...bringing your chin toward your chest...down...down...allow the muscles on the back of your neck to lengthen...allow your head to hang forward, gently stretching the muscles...breathing slowly in and out...

Now raise your chin and look straight ahead again.

Breathe in as you look up...up...raise your chin up as you gaze toward the ceiling...as you exhale, feel the muscles along the front of your neck lengthen in a pleasant stretch...and relax.

Relax your head backward and continue to look toward the sky. Breathe in and out. Stretch and relax.

Now return your head to a neutral position, facing forward.

Breathe in...

Look down one more time. Exhale as you allow the weight of your head to gently stretch the muscles of your neck, as you relax your head forward...no force is needed to assume this position...just relax into this position of looking down with your chin toward your chest...continue breathing gently as you feel your neck muscles relaxing further...no longer able to remain tightened or tense...

Return to neutral, facing forward...

And now, inhale as you look up again...relax your head back...feel the length of your neck, stretching out your muscles gently. Exhale.

Return to neutral.

Inhale...bring your shoulders up toward your ears. Raise them up high... and then lower your shoulders as you exhale.

Raise your shoulders again in a shrug...and lower them, allowing the muscles down the sides of your neck and the top of your shoulders to lengthen and give up the tension they were holding.

Roll your shoulders in forward circles...rotate...rotate...rotate...and now change directions...circle your shoulders back...rotate...rotate...rotate your shoulders.

Rest your shoulders now. Feel how much more relaxed your shoulders feel.

Now breathe in through your mouth as you stretch your jaw by opening your mouth wide...as wide as you can...feel the muscles stretching...exhale and relax...close your mouth, but let your jaw drop slightly so your teeth are not touching...let your jaw be loose and relaxed.

The last key area to stretch and relax to relieve tension is your hands. Clench your hands into tight fists...hold...and relax. Let your hands be limp.

Now open your hands wide...wider...stretching your fingers out wide... bring your arms forward and out to the sides, raising them above your head. Breathe in...and now breathe out as you relax your arms and hands, releasing the tension and letting them go limp. Shake out the tension as you gently shake both arms.

You have now stretched out the main areas where tension tends to accumulate. Proceed to stretch and relax further, moving from the feet upward.

Breathe in...and out...

Continue slow, gentle breathing.

Point your right toes, feeling the calf muscle tighten, and the front of your shin stretching. Now place your heel on the floor and bring your right foot toward your right shin to stretch the back of the lower leg. To stretch even further, lean slightly forward at the hips and bend your left leg to bring your center of gravity toward the floor. Feel the stretch up into your right hamstring.

Now release your right leg back to neutral and point your left toe. Stretch the muscles on the front of your left lower leg. Now put your left heel on the floor and point your left toes upward, stretching the back of the left lower leg. Lean forward a little, bending at the hips and right knee, to further stretch the calf and left hamstring.

Stretch...and relax. Release your left leg to neutral.

Breathe in...and out...

To stretch the thigh muscles, support yourself by placing your left hand on a wall, chair back, or other stable surface, and then bend your right knee and grasp your right foot behind you in your hand. Feel the quadriceps on the front of your thigh stretching. Hold...and now release. Slowly place your right foot back on the floor. Switch sides. Bend your left knee and grasp your left foot behind you in your hand. Stretch the front of the left thigh. Hold...and release.

With both feet on the floor, shoulder width apart, and hands on your hips, breathe in. Now exhale as you lean gently left...only until you feel a slight stretch at your waist on the right side. Hold...and now inhale and return to the center.

Now breathe out as you lean slightly to the right...feel a gentle stretch on your left side. Hold...and now inhale and release. Exhale.

Breathe in...and out...

Now gently grasp your hands behind you, with your arms straight. Breathe in as you bring both hands toward the back, away from the body. Bring your shoulder blades in toward each other. Feel the space between your collarbones widening and stretching. Hold this...stretch and relax...and now let go. Breathe out. Shake it out. Shake both arms gently and feel them relax.

Breathe in...gently and slowly curve your spine by leaning your head forward and down...breathe out as you tighten your abdominal muscles and feel your back making a slight C-shape. Now breathe in as you return to neutral. Feel the neutral S-curve of your spine. Exhale. Now inhale and look up toward the ceiling. Arch your back slightly—just a little—exaggerating the curve in your lower back a bit. Exhale and return to neutral.

Breathe in...and out as you tighten your abdominal muscles again, curving your back forward...and then relax. Breathe in...and out. Return to neutral. Let your back be relaxed with its natural curves. Stretch and relax.

Take a breath as you reach your right arm up toward the ceiling, stretch high up, lengthening the entire right side of your body. Breathe out and relax. Return to neutral. Now inhale and reach your left hand up high, reaching for the ceiling, lengthening the left side of your body. Then exhale and return to neutral.

Breathe in...and out...

Continue to breathe slowly and gently.

Bring your right arm across the front of your body, grasp your upper arm with your left hand, and gently stretch your right shoulder. Now relax. Bring your left arm across, grasp the upper arm with your right hand, and stretch your left shoulder. Now relax. Shake both arms a bit and feel them relax further.

Breathe in...stretch both arms straight forward...breathe out...reach straight out to the sides at shoulder level...inhale and reach forward again...exhale and stretch your arms back out to the sides...now inhale and reach up above your head...stretch and relax as you exhale. Shake your arms out.

Scan your body for any areas of tension. Gently stretch and relax these areas or focus on relaxing them passively, just by thinking about releasing the tension.

Breathe in...and exhale any remaining tension...

Breathe in...and release tension as you breathe out...

Stretch your arms up above your head as you breathe in...

Relax as you breathe out...

Stretch up...breathe in...

Relax...breathe out...

Breathe in...and out...

In...and out...

Allow your whole body to feel relaxed.

A Relaxing Walk

This relaxation script will guide you to take a relaxing walk—not just in your mind, but actually physically walking to relax.

In this script, I will describe going outside for a walk, but you may walk indoors or outdoors. You can walk on the spot, on a treadmill, back and forth in a room, around the block...take as short or as long a walk as your situation and the weather permit.

Begin reading the script here:

Begin by preparing for your relaxing walk. Ensure that you have suitable clothing for the weather and are wearing supportive footwear.

Throughout this exercise, monitor your body. Stop or ease up if you experience pain or discomfort. Keep all physical movements gentle, smooth, and relaxed.

Standing still in one place, take a deep breath in...and exhale.

Raise your arms above your head as you breathe in again...and lower your arms as you exhale.

Breathe slowly, deeply, and naturally as you do a few gentle stretches.

Keep your legs straight and bend forward. Place your hands on your knees. Feel the stretch in the back of your legs. Stretch further by placing your hands on your shins...reach down all the way to your ankles if you are able. Hold this stretch.

Slowly return to an upright position. Shake your right leg gently, shaking out the tension. Shake your left leg.

Raise your arms out to the sides at shoulder height. Keep your arms straight out beside you...now turn your body slightly at the waist to look to the right. Face forward again. Now turn at the waist to face slightly to the left. Return to the center.

Now lower your arms and shake them gently to shake out the tension.

Gently stretch any areas that feel especially tense.

When you are ready to proceed with your walk, go ahead and begin. Walk at whatever pace is comfortable for you. Not too slow...but not rushing either. Walk comfortably.

Focus your attention on the rhythm of your steps.

Left foot...right foot...left...right...

Allow this rhythm to soothe and relax you.

Continue on this relaxing walk. Enjoy the movement of your body. Feel your body becoming energized as your muscles move. Feel your limbs moving.

You can meditate as you walk by focusing your attention again on your footsteps. Count your steps as each foot touches the ground. One, two, three, four, one, two, three, four, one, two, three, four, one, two, three, four...

As your attention wanders, direct your focus again to your footsteps... one, two, three, four...

Continue to focus on your footsteps.

Feel your energy increase with each step. When each foot touches the ground, feel the energy rising all the way from your feet, up through your legs...your hips...body...arms...all the way to the top of your head.

The slight vibration when your foot lands on the ground serves to increase your relaxation and help you feel calm and energized.

Your legs feel strong, supporting the weight of your body. Notice the slight weight shifts that allow you to walk...from heel, to the front of your foot, and then transferring to the heel of the other foot, the front of that foot...back to the first foot...notice these weight shifts.

Notice the ever-repeating pattern of your steps. It is almost as if your feet are a wheel, rolling and rolling. One part contacts the earth while the other part is in the air. If time slowed down, you would notice that almost imperceptibly, the weight shifts from one part of the wheel to the next, and the next, and the next...until what was the bottom of the wheel is now the top. No part of the imaginary wheel...and no part of your feet...remains on the ground for long before transferring the weight to another part of your feet. Continuous motion.

Continue the relaxing walk.

The motion is very relaxing. Imagine the rhythm of your feet...it is like waves...flowing in and out...ever repeating...

Allow your breath to flow smoothly, also ever-repeating like waves...in... and out...in...out...

Hear the sounds of your footsteps. This is a calming and relaxing rhythm...just listening to this repeated beat. Notice all the repeated rhythms...footsteps...heartbeat...breathing...this smooth cycle of rhythms that allows you to continue forward at a leisurely walk.

Turn your attention now to your surroundings. Notice the environment around you...the surface you are walking on...the temperature...the colors...sounds...smells...enjoy your surroundings...enjoy this relaxing walk.

I'll end this script now, but you can continue to enjoy this relaxing walk for as long as you wish, feeling alert, refreshed, relaxed, and invigorated.

Progressive Muscle Relaxation with Keywords

Progressive muscle relaxation involves progressively tensing and then relaxing muscles to induce the relaxation response. This progressive relaxation script includes the keywords *breathe* and *relax*.

Begin reading the relaxation script here:

To begin this relaxation exercise, find a comfortable position where you can relax your muscles, such as lying down or sitting in a supportive chair.

This progressive muscle relaxation exercise should not cause pain or discomfort. If you experience discomfort when tensing your muscles, stop or ease up. Listen to your body, and make sure that you remain comfortable for the duration of this exercise.

When you are ready to begin, close your right hand into a fist. Squeeze tightly, feeling the tension in the muscles of your hand and lower arm. Hold as you breathe in...and relax, breathing out. Let all the tension go.

Now tighten your left hand into a fist, squeezing tightly. Feel the muscles of your hand and lower arm as they are very tense. Breathe in, holding the tension...and relax. Breathe out.

Concentrate now on your shoulders. Raise them up toward your ears, holding your arms tight against your sides. Tense the muscles of your upper arms and your shoulders. Hold that tension...breathe in...and relax. Breathe out, letting all the tension go.

Notice the difference in how your muscles feel. Notice what it feels like for your muscles to be tense, and what it feels like to be relaxed. Progressive muscle relaxation allows you to see how a relaxed muscle differs from a tense muscle.

Turn your attention to the muscles of your face. Tighten the muscles of your face by squeezing your eyes shut tightly and holding your lips tightly together. Feel the tension in the muscles of your face.

Hold...breathe in...and relax. Breathe out. Let your face relax and become limp.

Tighten the muscles of your jaw now, holding your teeth together tightly. Breathe in. Hold...and relax. Breathe out. Let your jaw drop loosely, calm and relaxed.

Proceed now to the muscles of your back. Arch your back slightly and pull your shoulder blades together, tightening the muscles of your back. Hold this tension. Breathe in, continuing to hold the tension...and exhale. Let all the tension go. Let the muscles of your back relax. Allow these muscles to be loose and comfortable.

Focus on the muscles of your chest and stomach. Bend forward slightly and cross your arms in front of you, tightening your chest and stomach muscles. Hold the tension...breathe in...and breathe out, relaxing, letting go. Feel the muscles relaxing.

Notice the feeling of tense and then relaxed. See the difference between these two states.

Tighten now the muscles of your buttocks, feeling your body raise up slightly as you do so. Hold the tension, feeling the tension in the muscles. Breathe in...hold...and relax. Breathe out. Let the muscles become relaxed and loose. Let all the tension go.

Focus your attention on the muscles of your thighs. Tighten these muscles on the front, sides, and back of your upper legs. Hold...breathe in...and now breathe out. Let the tension leave your body as you exhale.

Now tense the muscles on the front of your lower legs by raising your feet, pointing your heels down and your toes upward. Breathe in, holding the tension. Now breathe out. Relax.

Point your toes now and feel the tension in the back of your lower legs and in your feet. Hold this position tightly. Feel the tension. Breathe in...and exhale. Allow your muscles to relax. Feel the relaxation.

Notice the muscles throughout your body. Taking note of the difference between tension and relaxation, find any remaining areas of tension in your body. Focus on one area of tension as you breathe in. Hold that breath, imagining the tension is held with the air in your lungs. As you breathe out, let the tension go. Feel the area relaxing.

You can use this method to relax any areas of your body that remain tense. Scan your body now for any areas of tension, and focus on relaxing each area as you breathe.

(Pause)

If there are any remaining areas that are still tense, tighten the muscles in this area. Hold the tension tighter, tighter...breathe in...and relax. Feel the area relaxing as you breathe out. Notice the difference between tension and relaxation. See how you can create relaxation at will.

Let your body relax even further...deepening the state of relaxation. With each breath, you can become even more relaxed. More and more relaxed. Deeper and deeper, very deeply relaxed.

Peaceful...comfortable...relaxed...free from tension...no cares...no worries...just relaxation...

Enjoy this feeling of relaxation you are experiencing.

(Pause)

Take note of this feeling of relaxation. Memorize this feeling, so in the future you can picture this relaxed state and feel calmer simply by remembering how relaxed you were. Take a moment now to observe the relaxation you are experiencing and memorize it.

(Pause)

Now it is time to reawaken your body, but you can return to this relaxed state again, simply by remembering the difference between tension and relaxation. You can consciously relax your muscles and achieve a calm state of relaxation whenever you need to.

For now, turn your attention to your body, feeling your body reawaken. Feel the energy flowing through your body as your muscles reawaken, but remain free of tension. Gently move your muscles as you feel a state of wakefulness returning.

Take a few moments to continue to reawaken your mind and body, feeling your mind returning to its usual level of alertness.

When you are ready, open your eyes, and return to your day, feeling calm and energetic.

Calm Stretching Relaxation

This calm stretching relaxation will guide you to relax with a brief stretching routine.

Begin reading the relaxation script here:

Begin by finding a seated position. You may wish to sit on the floor or in a firm chair.

Listen to your body throughout this exercise. None of the stretches should cause pain. If you experience discomfort, stop or ease up.

Take a deep breath in...hold...and breathe out.

Breathe in...hold...and out.

In...hold...out.

Keep breathing slowly and deeply throughout this calm stretching relaxation.

With your knees bent slightly, place your hands on your thighs. Breathe in. As you exhale, lean forward, reaching your hands to your knees. Pause here as you breathe slowly, allowing a feeling of relaxation to begin. Hold this gentle stretch.

Breathe in...now exhale and lean forward further, reaching your hands to your lower legs. Remember to keep breathing. Reach your hands as far as you can comfortably stretch...all the way to your feet if you are able. Hold the stretch, breathing calmly. Feel the tension leaving your body as you stretch.

Slowly lean back toward neutral, moving your hands to your knees. Pause here. Breathe in...and out. Continue to breathe calmly as you return to an upright seated position.

Reach your arms out to the sides, straight out from the shoulder. Breathe in. Now turn your upper body as you exhale, looking to the right. Your left arm will point forward and your right arm will point to the back.Breathe in as you return to center. Keep your arms out at shoulder height. Pause here as you exhale. Take another breath in, and as you breathe out, turn to face to the left, pointing your right arm forward and your left arm back. Inhale as you return to center. Exhale, lowering your arms to your sides.

Relax here for a moment. Enjoy this calm stretching relaxation.

Lower your head forward, bringing your chin toward your chest. Simply let the weight of your head create the stretch, with no force or effort from you. Just relax, letting your head hang forward comfortably. Remember to continue breathing.

Now look up, leaning your head back. Look toward the sky.

Return to neutral, facing forward.

Turn your head now to the left...back to the center...and to the right... return to the center.

Lower your left ear toward your left shoulder...return to the center...and lower your right ear toward your right shoulder...return to the center.

Inhale as you bring your shoulders up toward your ears...and exhale as you let them drop back to neutral. Repeat, inhale...raising your shoulders. Exhale, lowering your shoulders.

Inhale...reach forward...stretch your arms forward as you exhale. Breathe in, reaching up above your head. Lower your arms as you breathe out.

Raise your arms above your head again as you breathe in...and lower them as you breathe out.

Relax for a moment in a neutral position, breathing calmly and deeply.

Now tuck your knees into your chest, reaching your arms around your legs. Sit like this for a moment, hugging your knees.

Place your hands at your sides. Breathe in. Now stretch your legs out to the front, pointing your toes, as you breathe out.

Now relax into a comfortable, neutral position.

Feel the relaxation in your body...feeling calm and relaxed...heavy...loose and relaxed.

(Pause)

Take a few moments now to mentally scan your body, noticing any areas that remain tense.

You can use calm stretching relaxation to relax any remaining areas of tension. Choose one area, and stretch, lengthening the muscles. Relax as you finish the stretch and return to neutral. Choose one more area that needs to relax. Stretch...and relax, returning to neutral.

Simply sit quietly now for a moment, noticing the feeling of relaxation you are experiencing. Feel the relaxation flowing through your body. Just relax.

(Pause)

Now that you have completed this calm stretching relaxation, you can return to your day feeling calm.

Take a moment to reorient yourself to your surroundings. Breathe in... and out...reawakening.

Keep breathing calmly. When you are feeling alert, you can return to your usual activities, keeping with you a calm and relaxed feeling.

Relaxation to Decrease Jaw Clenching

TMJ, teeth grinding, jaw clenching, and tension can all lead to jaw pain that interferes with sleep and with everyday life. This relaxation script will help to decrease clenching of the jaw by guiding you to release the muscles that lead to jaw tension, and will guide you to fall asleep free from tension.

Areas where tension tends to build need to be relaxed often, deliberately, to undo the habitual tensing that occurs. During this relaxation script, I will remind you several times to release the tension in your jaw and reduce jaw clenching.

It is normal if you find at first that your jaw relaxes and then gets tense again. Jaw clenching can recur several times while you are relaxing, but the reminders will help you to teach your body to relax this area. By relaxing over and over, jaw clenching can be decreased eventually by creating a new habit of relaxed muscles.

Begin reading the script here:

Let's begin the relaxation to decrease jaw clenching. Get comfortable, finding a position that will allow you to relax and go to sleep. Adjust your position as needed to allow yourself to start to relax.

You may want to close your eyes.

Take a deep breath in, through your nose. Exhale fully through your mouth.

Breathe in...and slowly out.

In...and out.

In...and out.

In...out.

Keep breathing slowly like this, smooth...deep breaths.

Allow your breathing to calm and center you.

As you breathe calmly, you can turn your attention gradually from the external to the internal.

Start by observing your external environment. The sounds around you...the room you are in...the feel of your clothes on your body...the surface you are on. Take in the details of your surroundings.

Now start to turn your attention inward. Notice your body...your thoughts...focus completely on your internal world. If you were to rate the physical tension you are experiencing right now, overall, what number would you rate the tension at, between zero and ten?

Where in your body is the tension stored? Do you have one area that is the most tense? How about the least tense? Where is your body the most relaxed? Just spend the next few moments focusing on how you are feeling right now.

(Pause)

Focus specifically now on your jaw. Is there any jaw clenching happening right now? Don't try to change this yet—just observe.

Now let the tension go, and allow your jaw to slacken. Does your jaw feel more relaxed now?

This time, tense your jaw, just a little. Hold your teeth together with just enough pressure that you can feel a slight tension in the muscles of your jaw. Do not tighten to the point of discomfort. Simply maintain a comfortable, steady pressure. Notice how the muscles on the sides of your face and jaw are tight, firm, and tense. Hold this mild tension for a few moments, noticing how it feels.

Now allow some of the tension to leave, very slowly...so slowly, your jaw is becoming ever so slightly more relaxed. Let your muscles get a little softer...a bit looser...until your teeth are still touching, but with no pressure at all. You almost cannot tell if your teeth are in contact with each other, because they are touching so lightly.

Notice how the muscles of your jaw are maintaining some tension. They are still firm because they are keeping a hold on your jaw, this very specific amount. Observe this state...your jaw is not yet relaxed, the muscles are holding onto some tension, but your jaw is not tight. This very specific jaw clenching is not comfortable or relaxed, but not painful either. A neutral state of moderate tension.

Now tense your jaw again, so that you are holding your teeth together with some pressure. The muscles of your jaw are tight, but not too tight. Tense, but not painful. Hold this tension, feeling how tight the muscles hold your jaw...clenching firmly.

And now, relax, letting the tension leave your jaw all at once, so completely that your lower jaw drops lower until your teeth are not touching. It is as if your lower jaw is simply floating. Your muscles are completely loose...feel the free, relaxed feeling in the muscles of your face and jaw.

You may even feel your lips part slightly, allowing your jaw to just hang loosely. No jaw clenching at all.

Now open your mouth wider, as wide as is comfortable. You might even want to yawn. Stretch the muscles of your face and mouth as you open your mouth wide.

Now relax, letting your mouth close loosely and comfortably. You will be holding your mouth now in a relaxed position, no jaw clenching at all, with your teeth slightly apart, your lips barely touching, and your muscles loose and relaxed.

This is the way your body can learn to hold your jaw. From this point forth, when you hear the phrase "relax your jaw," you can comfortably and easily let your lower jaw hang loosely in this position.

Take a moment to notice this feeling of relaxation in your jaw.

(Pause)

Now let's relax the rest of your body. Starting at the top of your head, allow a feeling of relaxation to grow. Feel your scalp relaxing first, a tingly feeling of relaxation that spreads down...to your forehead and the back of your head...the sides of your head and your ears...moving down now, down your face...eyes, nose, mouth, chin.

Your cheeks feel very relaxed. Loose, limp and relaxed. Feel your lips softening and relaxing...completely letting go of tension.

Feel the relaxation continue, letting your neck and shoulders relax. As your shoulders lower into a relaxed position, feel your jaw relaxing too. Relax your jaw. Lower your jaw and your shoulders together, relaxing them both. Feel the muscles completely giving up their hold.

The feeling of relaxation continues. Feel your upper back relaxing. Feel your chest relaxing as well, all the way from your shoulders and collar bones, down to the bottom of your ribcage and your sides.

Feel your middle back relax...the muscles letting go, relaxing completely. Let your stomach, sides, and lower back relax as well. Feel the relaxation through the core of your body. Warm and heavy. Calm and relaxed.

Allow your arms to relax, becoming very heavy. Feel any tension from your upper body flowing from your shoulders, down your arms, all the way to your hands, and draining out your finger tips and away.

Your arms relax from the shoulders, to your upper arms, elbows, lower arms, wrists, and hands. Your arms are very heavy and relaxed.

Relax your jaw. Let the muscles loosen and give up their hold. No tension. No jaw clenching. Simply relaxed and loose. Relax.

Now let your lower body relax. The area of your hips relaxes as you feel the relaxation moving from your lower back and down...all the way to your upper legs...your knees...lower legs...and feet.

Feel any remaining tension flow out through your toes, draining away, leaving your body...leaving only a feeling of relaxation and calm. Your legs are very heavy and relaxed.

Your whole body is relaxed now. Allow the relaxation to deepen. Relax your jaw. Floating...relaxing.

Just relax now, luxuriating in this calm, peaceful feeling.

(Pause)

Relax your jaw. Deliberately let your lower jaw drop into a free, relaxed position. Relax any other areas in your body that are tense. Feel all the tension just draining away...a feeling of deep relaxation remains. Calm...peaceful...relaxed.

(Pause)

Over the next few moments, you can just relax and rest as you fall asleep. Allow yourself to drift off as you become more and more deeply relaxed. Relax your jaw once more, feeling the complete relaxation there as you relax even more deeply.

A sleepy feeling of heaviness spreads throughout your body...feel yourself sinking into the surface you are on...sinking deeper...softly surrounded by relaxation.

Your arms are so heavy...and your legs are very heavy. Even your thoughts are heavy...relaxed...deeply relaxed and calm.

You are so warm...so sleepy...as if everything is slowing down...so peaceful...so calm...

Relaxing ever more deeply.

(Pause)

I'll count now from one to five. When I reach five you will be deeply asleep. Feel yourself drifting off to sleep, closer and closer to deep sleep with each number.

One...

Two...

Three...

Four...

Five.

Progressive Relaxation

Progressive relaxation is the process of relaxing muscles progressively throughout your body. This script will guide you to use a combination of observing the state of your body, tensing and then relaxing muscles, and passive progressive muscle relaxation.

Begin reading the script here:

To begin, find a comfortable position with your back supported. Choose a position that you can maintain for about half an hour, one that will allow you to completely relax.

Take a deep breath in...hold...and breathe out completely.

Breathe in again...hold...now exhale, releasing all the air.

Breathe in...and out...

In...out...

Continue breathing slowly and deeply. Feel your breathing start to relax your body.

Observe your body now, without trying to change anything. Simply notice how your body feels, with an attitude of curiosity and observation, free from judgment. Simply observe.

(Pause)

Now let's begin to relax your muscles. Start with your right hand. Close this hand into a fist, tightening the muscles of your right hand and forearm. Hold...tighter...feeling the tension...breathe in...and release. Breathe out. Let the muscles of your right hand and forearm relax. Notice the feeling of relaxation...and how it differs from tension.

Now make a fist with your left hand, tightening the muscles of your left hand and forearm. Squeeze...tighter...tighter...breathe in...and relax. Breathe out. Let all the tension go. Feel how relaxed the muscles of your left hand and forearm are now.

Focus now on your shoulders and upper arms. Bend both arms at the elbow, and tighten the muscles of your upper arms and shoulders. Hold this tension...raising your shoulders up toward your ears...tighter... breathe in as you hold the tension...and relax. Breathe out. Release all the tension, and let the muscles of your arms and shoulders relax.

Lower your arms to your sides, and let your shoulders drop into a relaxed position. Feel the difference between tension and relaxation. Feel your shoulders relaxing...easing downward as you let the tension go.

Turn your attention now to your feet. Bend your toes, curling them under and tightening your feet. Breathe in. Hold this tension in your feet...and relax. Breathe out. Let the tension go, feeling your feet relax.

Point your toes up, toward your knees, tightening the muscles on the front of your lower legs. Hold this tension...tighter...breathe in...and relax. Breathe out. Now point your toes, tensing the muscles on the back of your lower legs. Hold...tighter...breathe in...holding the tension...and release. Breathe out. Let all the tension go as you relax your lower legs completely.

Now tense the muscles of your upper legs. Let the muscles on the front, sides, and back of your thighs be tight and tense. Hold the tension... hold...Breathe in...and relax. Breathe out. Let your upper legs relax completely.

Focus on the muscles of your face. Raise your eyebrows, tightening your forehead. Hold...hold...breathe in...and now relax. Breathe out. Lower your eyebrows so your forehead is relaxed and smooth.

Now clench your teeth together, and press your tongue to the roof of your mouth. Tighten your lips and jaw. Breathe in. Hold the tension... and relax. Breathe out. Let your jaw be limp and loose.

Tighten the muscles of your face by squeezing your eyes tightly shut, wrinkling your nose, and tensing your cheeks. Breathe in. Hold the tension in the muscles of your face...and release. Breathe out. Let the muscles of your face relax.

Now that you have used progressive muscle relaxation for several of the muscles in your body, you can further relax with passive progressive relaxation. This process involves passively relaxing your body, bit by bit, as you lie still.

Recall the difference between tension and relaxation, and notice how you are able to create a feeling of relaxation at will. You can use this ability to increase the relaxation in each part of your body.

As your thoughts wander, you can notice these thoughts and allow them to pass. Keep an attitude of passive observation, not judging or adding to the thoughts that you have, simply noticing, and relaxing.

Begin at your feet. Turn your attention to this area. Just notice your feet right now...and notice a feeling of relaxation deepening, as your feet become even more relaxed.

Feel the relaxation spreading up to your ankles. Allow your ankles to become limp, loose, and relaxed.

Turn your attention to your lower legs. Notice your lower legs becoming more relaxed as the relaxation increases in this area, without any effort from you.

Simply enjoy the feeling of relaxation working its way through your body...calming and relaxing you.

Focus on your knees. Feel the relaxation spreading to your knees. They feel limp, loose, and relaxed.

Notice, now, your upper legs. Feel the relaxation in the front of your upper legs...the back of your upper legs...feel the outsides of your legs relaxing, and the insides of your legs becoming relaxed. Feel the relaxation throughout your upper legs. Feeling heavy and relaxed.

Your legs are limp and relaxed. Heavy...relaxed. It is a pleasant, calm sensation.

Allow the relaxation to continue, relaxing your hips and buttocks. Let all the tension go as you relax fully...allowing your pelvic area to relax... and your stomach.

Let your stomach become fully relaxed...loose...comfortable...free from tension.

Turn your attention to your lower back. Let the muscles there give up their hold and relax completely. Feel the relaxation in this area. Heavy and relaxed.

Now notice your sides. Feel the relaxation in your sides...as they become even more relaxed and loose. Letting go of tension completely.

Focus on your middle back. Feel the muscles letting go as they relax... loose and comfortable. Feel the relaxation...you are very calm and relaxed.

Turn your attention now to your upper back...feel your upper back relaxing...letting go...all the way to your shoulders.

Let your shoulders relax...allowing the relaxation to fill this area. Feel your shoulders, lowering slightly...as they offer no resistance to gravity...simply loose and relaxed. Comfortable.

Feel the relaxation in your hands and arms...feeling very warm and heavy. Pleasantly relaxed. All the way from your shoulders...to your upper arms, elbows, lower arms, and hands...feel the heaviness of relaxation filling your arms.

Focus now on your chest. Feel the relaxation spreading to your chest... filling your body...feel your calm, gentle breathing...very slow...very relaxed...each breath is so relaxed...

Allow your attention to focus now on your neck. Feel the relaxation as it continues, filling this area. Let the muscles of your neck give up their hold...relaxing the front of your neck...the back of your neck...the sides of your neck.

Feel the relaxation continuing...spreading throughout your body... pleasant, calm, and relaxed...up to your face and head. Feel the back of your head relaxing. Feel the relaxation in your ears...your jaw...cheeks... lips...chin...nose...eyes...eyebrows...forehead...all the way to the top of your head.

Your whole body is relaxed now. Relaxed and calm. Heavy. Peaceful. Relaxed.

Observe this feeling of relaxation. Enjoying the relaxation you are experiencing.

(Pause)

You are very deeply relaxed. Notice that the relaxation can become even deeper as you notice your breathing again. Feel yourself relaxing even more with each breath.

Each breath in is like breathing in relaxation...and each breath out allows you to let go of tension even more.

Breathing in relaxation...and relaxing more as you breathe out...

Continue breathing, noticing your breaths. Taking deep, cleansing breaths. Just notice your breaths, without trying to change anything. Simply relax and notice your breathing.

(Pause)

Observe this state of relaxation closely...memorizing the feeling of relaxation.

Know that you can return to this relaxed state at will.

(Pause)

Now that you have completed this relaxation exercise, you can slowly reawaken your mind and body...gradually becoming more alert.

Notice the environment around you...becoming more awake and alert.

Feel your mind and body reawakening.

Move your muscles a little...wiggle your fingers and toes...feeling your arms and legs wake up. Reawakening your body.

Almost completely awake now...

When you are ready, open your eyes, and sit quietly for a moment while you reawaken fully. When you return to your usual level of alertness and wakefulness, you can return to your usual activities, feeling full of energy and refreshed.

Anchoring Relaxation

"Anchoring" is an effective way to train your body to quickly relax by making an association in your brain between a state of relaxation and touching a specific spot on your hand or wrist. It is a conditioning of the relaxation response so that a neutral action results in relaxation.

Once you are relaxed, you will use anchoring to associate the action of squeezing your right thumb (or your chosen anchoring spot) with a state of relaxation. Once this association is made, you will be able to trigger relaxation quickly, simply by squeezing your right thumb.

Practice this script several times to firmly ingrain the association in your brain. Use this relaxation exercise at different times of day and in different locations for optimal learning.

After a few sessions, you will notice that the first time you squeeze your right thumb, you will become relaxed. When this occurs, you will know that the anchoring process has been successful, and you can then relax immediately just by squeezing your right thumb—any time, anywhere.

Choose a spot on your hand or wrist that will work as your "anchor." *Squeezing the right thumb* is the anchor I will describe in this script. Whatever spot you choose, consistently use the same location.

Choose an anchor word as well. I'll use "relax" as an example here, but you can use any word you like.

Begin reading the anchoring relaxation script here:

Now it is time to relax and begin the process of anchoring.

Begin by stretching out your muscles gently. Raise your arms above your head as you breathe in...and lower your arms to your sides as you exhale. Raise your arms and stretch as you breathe in again...relax and lower them as you breathe out.

Roll your shoulders forward...and back...now relax. Let the tension drain away from your shoulders.

Now that you have moved your shoulders and arms to allow your body to begin to release the tension it has been holding, find a comfortable and relaxed position sitting or lying down.

Stretch the muscles of your face as you open your mouth wide and breathe in...yawn if you wish...stretch the muscles of your face...and let your face slacken gently as you breathe out...relax completely...let your lower jaw hang loosely below your upper jaw, your teeth not touching.

Scan your body for areas of tension as you take another deep breath in. Feel the tension in your body as you hold that breath. Now let the tension go as you let the breath go.

Point your toes, stretching your legs. Release the muscles of your legs and relax. Now bring your feet upward, toward your shins, stretching the back of your legs. Release the stretch, relaxing your legs completely.

Let your legs become limp...loose and relaxed...

Let your arms become relaxed and loose...

Notice how your body feels.

Feel the relaxation flowing through your body. Notice that you can become even more relaxed...wiggle your toes once or twice, and then allow your toes to be still and relaxed.

Feel the relaxation flowing...spreading...until your feet are relaxed as well.

Let the relaxation continue to your ankles. Feel how loose and relaxed your ankles feel.

Now allow the muscles of your lower legs to give up their hold. Feel the relaxation in your lower legs...calm...relaxed...heavy...relaxed...

Enjoy the feeling of relaxation as it continues to your knees...then your upper legs...feel your thighs relaxing and letting go...your legs feel very heavy...very heavy, and very relaxed...

Feel the relaxation flowing...allow your buttocks to relax...your pelvic area...and now your abdomen...feel the muscles becoming loose and relaxed...letting go of all the tension...relaxed and heavy...

Allow your lower back to relax...feel the relaxation there as the muscles of your lower back give up their hold...leaving nothing but relaxation... calm...peaceful...

Let the relaxation continue to flow throughout your body, spreading now to the muscles of your sides...feel your sides, abdomen, and chest gently moving in and out with each breath...each breath making you even more relaxed...

Allow the muscles of your sides to let go...feel the relaxation filling your core...relaxing your chest and stomach...your middle back...your upper back...

The relaxation continues to increase...pleasantly more and more relaxed...deeper and deeper...feel your shoulders relaxing...your upper arms...your elbows...

Feel your arms relaxing more and more...becoming heavier and heavier...let the relaxation continue...spreading to your lower arms... your wrists...and your hands...

Your arms become completely limp and relaxed...pleasant...relaxed...

Let the relaxation continue from your lower back...middle back...and upper back...to your neck...the back of your neck and the front of your neck...the back of your head...the top of your head...your chin...your face...your jaw...

Feel your cheeks relaxing...becoming completely loose and relaxed...feel your lips relaxing...becoming soft and relaxed...let your tongue relax... feel your nose relaxing...let your eyes relax...your eyelids are very heavy and relaxed...feel your eyebrows relaxing...and your forehead becoming smooth, cool, and relaxed...

Your whole body is now fully relaxed...

Enjoy the relaxation you are experiencing...use your left thumb and two fingers to gently squeeze your right thumb, while at the same time saying silently, "relax,"anchoring the feeling of relaxation to this spot.

Experience the feeling of deep relaxation. Notice your breathing. Notice how calm and regular your breathing is...watch your breathing, without trying to change it in any way.

As you breathe in, say in your mind, "I am relaxed."

As you breathe out, mentally say, "I am calm."

I am relaxed.

I am calm.

I am relaxed.

I am calm.

Now squeeze your right thumb while mentally saying, "relax." Let the anchoring occur as this spot becomes associated with the peaceful, relaxed state you are in.

Feel the relaxation deepen each time you squeeze your right thumb while saying, "relax."

Continue to allow the relaxation to flow throughout your body... calm...peaceful...relaxed...

(Pause)

Memorize this feeling of relaxation. Notice how your body feels. Notice how calm you are. Create a picture in your mind of this state of relaxation. With this image in mind, gently squeeze your right thumb one more time while saying to yourself, "relax." Feel the relaxation deepen.

This spot is an anchor to remind you of the relaxation you are feeling right now. In the future, when you squeeze your right thumb, the feelings and memories of how relaxed you are right now will fill your mind, and your body will automatically relax.

You are as relaxed as you want to be. Calm...relaxed...

Warm...safe...comfortable...relaxed...

(Pause)

Now it is time to start to become aware of your surroundings and return to your usual level of alertness. Keep your eyes closed for a few moments while your body reawakens.

You can use anchoring any time to cue your body to relax. Remember the pleasant, peaceful state of relaxation, and know that your anchor can remind you of the relaxation you experienced.

Count up, from one to five with me, becoming more alert with each number, until at five you are fully awake and alert.

One, becoming more awake, more alert, energetic...

Two, feeling calm, awakening even more...

Three, almost totally awake now, ready to resume with your day...

Four, eyes open, stretch the muscles, becoming completely awake...

Five, fully awake, fully alert, rested and ready to go.

Creative Relaxation Scripts

Creative Expression Relaxation

This script guides you to use drawing to calm the mind. You will create two abstract drawings, one on each side of a piece of blank paper.

Start reading the creative expression relaxation script here:

Begin by placing a blank sheet of paper and a box of colored pencils on a clean tabletop. Play music that you find relaxing, calming, or energizing. The type of music you select is up to you.

Sit down at the table. Place your hands, palms down, on the table top. Close your eyes, and take a deep breath in...and now exhale slowly, releasing the tension in your body.

Picture the tension in your body and the stressful thoughts in your mind. If this stress were a color, what color might it be?

Open your eyes and select the color, or colors, of your stress from the box of colored pencils.

Allow the creative expression relaxation to begin as you place the tip of the pencil anywhere on the paper, and begin to move your hand and arm. Scribble out the tension. Scribble away the stress. It doesn't matter what the scribble looks like. Allow the lines and shapes you are drawing to represent your stress and tension.

Feel the movement of your arm releasing the stress and tension onto the paper. Feel the tension in your body moving down your upper arm, lower arm, wrist, and hand...through your fingers, and into the pencil. The stress and tension of your day are held inside the pencil, and as the pencil contacts the paper, the tension, stress, and worries are left behind on the page.

Keep moving the pencil across the page. You may choose to change colors, or use more than one pencil at the same time. You may want to draw with both hands. Keep moving. Keep filling the paper with marks, shapes, and lines.

Feel the tension draining from your body and out onto the paper.

Continue this exercise until you feel like some of the tension has left your body, or until what you see on the paper to represent your stress is complete.

(Pause)

When you are finished drawing your stress, turn over the paper.

Now imagine that on the top of your head is a string, holding you gently upright. Imagine the string tightening, lengthening your spine until your back is straight. Feel your shoulders lowering slightly as the muscles in your neck and back become smooth and relaxed. Keep your posture upright and straight, but not rigid. Maintain the natural curves in your spine.

Breathe in again, drawing in a deep, relaxing breath...

Breathe out tension...

Breathe in relaxation...

And breathe out tension...

Allow each part of your body to relax. Picture the feeling of relaxation rising from your feet, all the way to your head. Allow your feet to relax. Feel your legs becoming warm and heavy. Relax your hips, stomach, back, and chest. Relax your arms and shoulders. Relax your neck. Relax your face and head.

Breathe in relaxation...

Breathe out tension...

Breathe in, I am calm...

Exhale, I am relaxed...

I am calm...

I am relaxed...

(Pause)

Picture this feeling of calm and relaxation in your mind. If this tranquility were a color, what color might it be?

Select the color or colors that represent this serenity.

Allow the pencil you have chosen to contact the paper. Feel the relaxation flowing throughout your body. Begin to move the pencil in a gentle, calm rhythm. Use the movement of drawing, and the feel of drawing, to express the relaxation.

As the relaxation flows across the page, notice that your mind is becoming tranquil and relaxed. Focus on the movement of your body. Notice the tip of the pencil moving along the paper smoothly. See the calm markings left on the page. Feel the creative expression relaxation flowing through your body and your mind.

Allow yourself to be totally focused on, and absorbed in, the creative process. Create a picture of the expression of relaxation. Feel the relaxation as you see the relaxation developing on the page.

(Pause)

Feel tension flowing out through the pencil, and relaxation flowing in with each movement of the pencil on paper. As your drawing grows, the feeling of relaxation increases.

Enjoy your creativity.

Allow your creative expression and relaxation to flow.

(Pause)

Draw or scribble freely. Allow your body to move calmly, unrestricted, as you experience the relaxation of creativity. Free yourself from expectations about the work you are creating. It doesn't matter what it looks like. Appreciate the process. Experience creativity. Embrace relaxation and revitalization.

Breathe in relaxation...

Breathe out tension...

Breathe in relaxation...

Draw away tension...

Draw in relaxation...

Draw out relaxation...

Draw in relaxation...

Draw relaxation...

Draw relaxation...

Continue to draw for as long as you wish.

Music Relaxation

The purpose of this music relaxation script is to find out how different styles of music affect your mood and energy level. This is an expressive media exercise (using media for self expression).

Here are three media options for how to express your response to the music during this music relaxation script: crayons, clay, or audio. This way you can decide if you want to respond in a visual, kinesthetic, or auditory way.

Option 1: Paper and crayons. Get a large blank sheet of paper, or several smaller sheets. You will also need a box of crayons with at least five different colors.

Option 2: Clay or dough. You can make inexpensive dough (that can air dry or be dried in the oven and is hard enough to paint afterward— great for making ornaments) with one cup of salt, two cups of flour, and one cup of water.

Option 3: Audio recordings of your voice. Record yourself as you listen to the relaxation script.

Listen to each music clip in this music relaxation script. As you listen, use your chosen media to express how you feel in response to the music.

If you have chosen crayons, use the crayons to draw, scribble, or write on the paper. Make marks to describe your response to the music. You can use color, texture, pressure, shape, lines, written words, or any other form of expression to record your experience during the music relaxation script.

If you selected dough, shape the dough as you listen to each clip. You can use texture, shape, pressure, movement, or any other form of expression by moving the dough in your hands as you listen to each music clip.

If you chose audio recordings, you can use sounds, humming, tapping, spoken words, or any other kind of auditory expression in response to the music clips. You may choose to record the track number, record your response, pause the recording, and record any further responses (rather than recording the entire script). This will make it easier to review your responses quickly at the end.

(Pause to select materials)

Now that you have selected your medium of choice, I will play short clips by introducing them only by number. Make sure that you have a way to review your responses so that you know which music track they are associated with. You might want to number each drawing, sculpture, or audio recording so they correspond to the track you were listening to.

After going through all 9 tracks, this script will discuss what the styles were and give you a chance to review your responses and determine how the different styles affected your energy and mood.

Ready? Let's begin.

Track 1.

(Play track)

End of track 1.

(And so on up to track 9)

End of track 9.

Now that you have listened to some different music and responded with your media of choice, I'll review what the tracks were and discuss the effects of music on mood and energy.

The clips I used are from _____. Here is the style of each clip:

Track 1: Song title, Style

(And so on to track 9.)

You probably noticed that you responded to the different tracks in a variety of ways:

- Some you may have liked, while others you might have disliked.
- Your energy level may have gone up or down.
- You may have felt emotional responses (happy, sad, angry, calm, energized, bored, annoyed, peaceful, etc).
- Some music might have helped you focus, other music may be distracting.
- Some styles help you feel more relaxed, while others less relaxed.

Review your work that you produced while listening to the music. Notice your responses.

What does this tell you about your musical preferences? What do your responses tell you about your music relaxation preferences?

Music for relaxation ideally will be:

- Non-distracting
- Calming
- Something that helps you feel peaceful
- Music you like

Maybe some of the clips you heard fit these criteria. Perhaps none of them did. Experiment with different kinds of music until you find something that fits.

Remember that you can use music in a variety of ways. Relaxation is one option, but you can also use music to increase your energy (for example, playing upbeat music when doing chores), vent emotions (such as sadness or anger), or improve your mood.

Each individual's preferences are unique. Once you have found a style of music that you prefer, you can play this music with relaxation scripts to enhance your relaxation experience.

Quick Relaxation Scripts

Quick Relaxation: Yawn and Stretch

This yawn and stretch relaxation script is a quick relaxation technique that you can do any time, anywhere to relax.

Begin reading the script here:

A yawn forces you to take a deep breath, slow down the breathing, and to exhale fully. This counteracts the fast shallow breathing experienced as a symptom of stress and anxiety.

Stretching is effective in lengthening the muscles—the opposite of short, tensed muscles. Here is a quick guided yawn and stretch.

Do you know how to yawn? Sure you do!

Try it...open your mouth wide, yawn loudly with a big sigh, and stretch your arms above your head.

Make sure to stretch out the back and shoulder muscles—key places where tension can build up.

Get ready by rotating your shoulders and shaking your shoulders and arms. This will help to loosen up tight muscles.

Now open your mouth, and start to breathe in.

Open your mouth wider...wider...and open the back of your throat.

Feel the breathing passages opening. Your ears may even pop.

Allow the yawn to arrive as you inhale, and then complete the yawn by breathing out loudly with a sigh.

Take a few slow, deep breaths. Breathe in...and out. In...and out. In...out.

Now yawn again, and as you inhale with your mouth open wide, stretch your arms out and up. Stretch your muscles as you yawn.

Allow your arms to drop back to your sides as you breathe out with a sigh.

Notice how much more relaxed and calm you feel.

Quick Relaxation: Deep Breathing

This deep breathing relaxation script explains why and how to use counting to slow your breathing.

Breathing is fundamental to survival. When we are stressed or anxious, our breathing changes in an attempt to allow the body to engage in intense physical activity for survival.

Breathing becomes more rapid, but unfortunately, it also gets shallow. We begin to breathe short, quick, shallow breaths.

Ever feel like you can't catch your breath? It isn't that you are not able to catch your breath, it's that you are not exhaling.

Short gasps of air inward are followed by very small exhalations. The feeling of not catching one's breath leads to even more inhalations...but still no complete exhale. The lungs are so full of old, stale air, new good air cannot enter. We sense the need for oxygen, and in panic, attempt to inhale even more.

The solution to this problem is clear: exhale!

Proper breathing is an excellent way to manage stress because it stops this negative cycle and calms the body.

Deep breathing not only helps to cure anxiety and stress, it also triggers relaxation.

Breathing too fast and deep causes lightheadedness and numbness or tingling of the extremities. Here is a way to slow down your breathing while keeping it deep and exhaling fully.

Inhale slowly to the count of four (count slowly; to the pace of one-one-thousand, two-one-thousand...). Pause to the count of three. Exhale slowly to the count of five. The breathing process goes like this:

Inhale...two, three, four...

Pause...two, three...

Exhale...two, three, four, five...

Inhale...two, three, four...

Pause...two, three...

Exhale...two, three, four, five...

Keep breathing at this slow, even pace.

Continue for a minute or two.

30-Second Relaxation

This script for quick relaxation will describe how to relax even though you are busy.

When you are short on time, it can be particularly challenging to make relaxation a regular part of your day. You might recognize the benefits of relaxing, but still can't find the time to sit down and actually practice relaxation techniques.

Quick relaxation is the solution. This allows you to set aside brief periods of time so you can relax throughout the day, even though you are busy.

Begin reading the relaxation script here:

Right now, take 30 seconds to relax your body and reduce stress.

Stand up or otherwise change positions.

Roll your shoulders forward...and now roll your shoulders back.

Clench your hands into fists...hold...and release.

Stretch your arms out and stretch your hands wide open, reaching up above your head. Spread your fingers wide. Reach your arms high.

Now relax your hands and lower your arms.

Lower your shoulders, away from your ears. Ease your shoulders back slightly.

Let your shoulders relax.

Relax your jaw by dropping the lower jaw slightly. Make sure your teeth aren't touching.

Now count silently as you breathe:

Inhale...two, three, four...

Pause...two, three...

Exhale...two, three, four, five...

Inhale...two, three, four...

Pause...two, three...

Exhale...two, three, four, five...

(Repeat until 28 seconds have passed.)

Change positions one more time, and then get back to your day!

Quick Progressive Muscle Relaxation Script: Key Areas

This is a quick progressive muscle relaxation script that will allow you to focus on key areas where stress can build up. Relax these areas as you go about your daily activities to prevent stress.

Tense and relax each area I mention. When you tense the area, do not cause any pain. Tighten only until you feel tension. If you feel any discomfort, stop or ease up.

The first key area is your neck and shoulders.

Raise your shoulders up toward your ears...tighten the muscles there... hold...feel the tension there...and now release. Let your shoulders drop to a lower, more comfortable position.

The next key area is your hands.

Tighten your hands into fists. Very, very tight...as if you are squeezing a rubber ball very tightly in each hand...hold...feel the tension in your hands and forearms...and now release. Shake your hands gently, shaking out the tension. Feel how much more relaxed your hands are now.

Now, your forehead.

Raise your eyebrows, feeling the tight muscles in your forehead. Hold that tension. Now tightly lower your eyebrows and scrunch your eyes closed, feeling the tension in your forehead and eyes. Hold it tightly. And now, relax...let your forehead be relaxed and smooth, your eyelids gently resting.

Your jaw is the next key area.

Tightly close your mouth, clamping your jaw shut, very tightly. Your lips will also be tight and tense across the front of your teeth. Feel the tension in your jaw. Hold...and now relax. Release all the tension. Let your mouth and jaw be loose and relaxed.

There is only one more key area to relax, and that is your breathing.

Breathe in deeply, and hold that breath. Feel the tension as you hold the air in. Hold...and now relax. Let the air be released through your mouth. Breathe out all the air.

Once more, breathe in...and how hold the breath. Hold...and relax. Release the air, feeling your entire body relax.

Breathe in...and out...

In...and out...

Continue to breathe regular breaths.

You have relaxed all the key areas where tension can build up. Remember to relax these areas a few times each day, using this quick progressive muscle relaxation script, to prevent stress symptoms.

Breathing Awareness

This breathing awareness relaxation script will guide you to focus on each stage of a breath as you breathe slowly and gently.

Let's begin. Throughout this breathing awareness exercise, breathe in this way:

Breathe in to the count of four, hold for the count of 3, and breathe out to the count of 5.

It goes like this:

Breathe in...2...3...4...hold...2...3...exhale...2...3...4...5...

Breathe in...2...3...4...hold...2...3...exhale...2...3...4...5...

Breathe in...2...3...4...hold...2...3...exhale...2...3...4...5...

Breathe in...2...3...4...hold...2...3...exhale...2...3...4...5...

Continue to breathe at this slow pace.

While you are breathing slowly, I'll direct your breathing awareness to different stages of the breath. Focus all of your attention on each stage I mention.

First, notice the breath as it enters your nose. Notice each time you breathe in, the way the breath feels on your nostrils.

Feel the breath as it passes through your nasal passages, and down behind your throat.

(Pause)

Where does the air go next? Feel each time you inhale, the breath passing down your windpipe.

Feel the breath going down...

Feel the breath going down...

(Pause)

Notice where the air enters your lungs. Allow your breathing awareness to deepen the feeling of relaxation you are experiencing.

Feel the air expand your lungs with each in breath.

Feel your lungs expand...and relax...expand...and relax...expand...and relax...

(Pause)

Now notice the exhalation phase of breathing. Observe as the air leaves your lungs and begins to travel upward. Focus your attention on that moment of each breath.

Now turn your attention to the breath traveling up and out, through your mouth. Feel the breath in your throat, your mouth, and across your lips.

Notice each breath as a whole now. See how the breaths flow like waves. Fist in...and then a pause...and out...and then a pause...notice the pauses, these rests between breaths.

Now as you relax...you can count your breaths as they continue to flow gently. Count ten breaths.

(Pause)

When you are finished counting your breaths, notice how calm and relaxed you are. See how regular your breathing has become...how calm your breathing is.

When you are ready to return to your day, you can reawaken your body and return to the present. I'll count to five. With each number, you can become more and more alert, reaching full alertness when I reach five.

One...

Two...

Three...

Four...

Five.

Quick and Easy Relaxation

This quick and easy relaxation is a method that you can use every day, at any time, to decrease the tension in your body and counteract the effects of stress. Rather than a conventional relaxation script, this is a summary of techniques that can be used for relaxing quickly, accompanied by instruction on how to use each technique.

Here are some quick ways to begin the relaxation response.

First, notice your breathing. Deep breathing is a quick and easy relaxation technique. When you breathe in, your entire chest and abdomen will expand outward. As you exhale, your sides, chest, and stomach move inward.

Focus on breathing slowly and on completely emptying the lungs with each breath. If you breathe slowly like this for a minute or two, your heart rate will begin to slow down, your mind will clear, and you will begin to relax.

Let's practice. Breathe in, deeply...pause for a moment...and now exhale fully.

Breathe in...and out...

In...out...

Keep breathing slowly and calmly.

Now, relax the areas in your body where tension tends to build.

The neck and shoulders are a common area where tension builds up. You can relax your shoulders by lowering them slightly. If you are not sure if your shoulders are more relaxed, raise them up toward your ears, and hold this position. Hold the tension...and then relax, lowering your shoulders.

You can repeat this a few times until you find that your shoulders are more relaxed and the muscles there are not holding on to tension.

To relax your neck, tip your head forward, bringing your chin toward your chest. Let your head hang loosely, without any pressure or effort at all. Just allow your head to hang forward, and feel the muscles on the back of your neck lengthening.

Muscles in a shortened position are tense, while muscles in a lengthened position are relaxed. Let the muscles of your neck lengthen, and then gently raise your head back to a neutral position. Lower your shoulders again, and feel how the neck and shoulder area is more relaxed.

Another area where tension can build is in the jaw. This can lead to headaches and jaw pain. To relax your jaw, allow your lower jaw to drop so your lower teeth and upper teeth are not touching. Your lips should be slightly apart or gently touching.

Tension may also build in the hands and arms because of clenched fists. To relax your hands and arms, open your hands wide, stretching the muscles. Straighten your arms as you do this, lengthening the muscles from your hands all the way to your elbows and shoulders. Then let your hands relax into a neutral position, allowing your hands and arms to relax completely.

You can even tighten your hands into fists, and hold the tension...and then release, feeling the muscles give up their hold.

Another way to relax your hands and arms is to shake your hands, as if you are shaking water off them. Shake your hands for several seconds. Now stop, and let your hands relax. Notice that they feel slightly tingly, and more relaxed. This shaking not only releases tension from the muscles, it increases blood flow to the hands.

When the body is tense, blood flow is directed to the large muscles and organs, and blood flow in the hands and feet is decreased. Hands and feet may feel cold when the body is stressed or tense. Relaxation causes hands and feet to warm up as circulation returns to normal. Shaking your hands can promote this type of blood flow and help to trigger the relaxation response.

You may have other areas where tension builds up. A feeling of pain or tightness will signal where the tension is stored in your body. Find any tense areas, and consciously relax the muscles, returning your posture to a neutral, relaxed position.

You can imagine that as you breathe in, you are directing your breath to this area, and as you breathe out, you are releasing tension from this area through your breath.

Continue this process of quick and easy relaxation until you are feeling less tense, more relaxed, and calm. For deep relaxation, you can continue the relaxation process by using progressive muscle relaxation, guided imagery, or other techniques. For everyday tension relief, this quick and easy relaxation will be effective in starting the relaxation response.

When you are feeling tense, remember to:

Breathe deeply and slowly.

Lower your shoulders.

Lengthen the muscles in your neck.

Relax your jaw.

Release tension from your hands and arms.

Focus on relaxing any other tense areas in your body.

You can do these steps in a matter of seconds, and use this quick and easy relaxation method whenever you are feeling stressed or tense.

Sleep Relaxation Scripts

Sleep Relaxation

Guided sleep relaxation is a natural sleep aid that will help you unwind and simply sleep. Listen to this relaxation script any time you need to drift easily into deep, healthy sleep.

Do you find that your mind is busy, and full of thoughts that keep you from going to sleep? This sleep relaxation script will allow you to put a time limit on the thinking you do before sleeping, and teach you how to quiet your mind and fall asleep.

You may wish to keep a notepad by your bed so you can quickly write down important things you must remember—once they are written down, you no longer need to worry about them and can sleep, knowing that you can review your notepad in the morning.

During the first part of the sleep relaxation script, you may wish to jot down important things that need to be done tomorrow. Any thoughts that are difficult for you to let go can be written down to deal with later. Remember that once you start to clear your mind for sleep, the notepad must be put away.

Begin reading the script here:

This guided sleep relaxation script will help you to fall into a deep, restful sleep.

Begin by lying on your back with your hands on your thighs or at your sides. You can change positions any time you need to in order to be more comfortable, but start by lying on your back for now.

Mentally scan your body for areas of tension. Make note of how your body feels. During this sleep relaxation session, you will focus on releasing any tension in your body, and on quieting the mind. Once the mind is calm and peaceful, you will easily drift into pleasant, restful sleep.

Breathe in, drawing in life-giving air and relaxation.

Exhale slowly, expelling any tension.

You might have thoughts about things you did today, or things you need to do tomorrow.

Perhaps you are worried about something or someone.

Now is the time to clear your mind for sleep, so tomorrow you will be refreshed and strong and can handle your duties and roles.

Now take a few moments to do the thinking you need to do before you sleep. Focus now on anything you need or want to think about before you go to sleep. For the next two minutes, do any worrying or thinking you decide to do.

Now it is time to clear your mind for sleep. There is nothing else you need to be doing at this moment. Nothing you need to be thinking, except calm, relaxed thoughts.

Notice how your body feels right now.

Where in your body is today's tension stored? Focus your attention on the part of your body that feels most tense. Focus in on one small area of tension. Breathe in deeply, and then let that tension go as you breathe out with a sigh.

Notice where your body feels most relaxed. Let that feeling of relaxation grow with each breath. Spreading further and further the feeling of relaxation.

(Pause)

Feel your attention drifting as you become sleepy and calm. For the next few moments, you can choose to focus on counting, and become more relaxed as each number passes through your mind. Concentrate your attention on the number one.

As you count from one to ten, you will become more deeply relaxed. As you relax, you can allow your mind to drift into pleasant, refreshing sleep.

Count slowly with me...one...focusing on the number one...

Two...you are more deeply relaxed...deeper and deeper...calm. Peaceful.

Three...feel the tension leaving your body...relaxation filling your body and mind. Concentrating just on the numbers.

Picture in your mind number four. Very relaxed. Calm...tingly feeling of relaxation in your arms and legs...very heavy...pleasantly heavy and relaxed.

Concentrating on number five...as you drift deeper...deeper. Calm. Sleep washing over you. Peaceful.

Six...deeply relaxed...

Seven...your body and mind are very calm...

Eight...so very pleasant and heavy...

Nine...allowing your mind to drift...easily...no direction...floating... relaxing...

Ten...you are deeply relaxed...

(Pause)

Now you may count back down from ten to one. When you reach one, you will be fully relaxed and drift into deep sleep. When I say start, slowly count on your own while I continue to talk.

Focus only on the numbers while I describe the relaxation experience. Start now at ten...and very slowly focus on nine...and keep going on your own...

...as you become deeply relaxed...warm...heavy...

Peaceful...comfortable...

Sleep...relaxation...

Pleasant and calm...

Drifting...

Drifting...

Accepting...

Sleep...

Relaxation...

Feeling very good and peaceful...

At peace with yourself...

Confident...

Nurturing...

Refreshing sleep...

(Pause)

Deeply relaxed...

Sleep deeply...

Calm and relaxed...

Quiet...

Sleep...relaxation...

Smooth, even breathing...

Warm and calm...

Relaxed...

Peaceful...

Relaxed...

(Allow voice to become quieter so words fade out)

Sleep relaxation...

Allowing yourself to drift into deep sleep...

Deep pleasant sleep relaxation...

Sleep...

Sleep Countdown

This sleep countdown is a guided relaxation script that will help you fall asleep. Focusing the mind allows you to decrease the thoughts that can interfere with falling asleep, and teach you how to allow thoughts to pass rather than dwelling on them and remaining alert.

Begin reading the sleep countdown relaxation script here:

Find a comfortable sleeping position. You can change positions if needed, but try not to move around very much.

Take a deep breath in, pause...and breathe out.

Wherever your body is tense, focus on relaxing the muscles.

Feel your shoulders relax and sink into the bed.

Allow your jaw to drop slightly.

Wiggle your toes once or twice and feel your feet and legs relaxing.

Gently open and close your hands once...and again...and then relax your hands and arms.

Take a deep breath in, feeling the tension in your chest and stomach as you hold that breath...and allow your chest and stomach to relax as the breath escapes slowly.

Notice any areas of tension in your body, and relax those areas now.

Your body will continue to relax...

The sleep countdown will start in a moment. Each number you count can allow you to feel more and more relaxed, and drift toward sleep.

Count very slowly, breathe with each count, and concentrate your mind on the numbers. As thoughts come up, you can disregard them and turn your attention back to the numbers.

Starting with 50, breathe in and silently count "50." Picture the number 50. Breathe out to the number 50.

Picture now the number 49. Breathe in. Noticing your eyelids. They might be feeling very heavy and comfortable. Exhale, counting 49.

48. See the number 48 in your mind's eye. Focusing all your attention on 48.

47. You might be feeling more relaxed. Even sleepy. Concentrating on 47.

46. Pleasant and calm. Breathing slowly and deeply.

45. Your attention drifts slowly, randomly...you can focus back on the numbers

44. You might be feeling very sleepy now. Pleasantly drifting off into sleep...

43. Calm. Relaxed. Peaceful. Safe.

42. Focusing only on the numbers. Allowing other thoughts to slip away.

41. Deeply relaxed. Deeper and deeper. See the numbers in your mind, slowly counting down to sleep.

40. Continue the sleep countdown on your own now. Concentrating just on the numbers. Continue to count down now.

As your attention wanders, allow your mind to drift back to focus just on the numbers as you count down to sleep.

(Pause)

Pleasantly drifting...

(Pause)

No direction except for down deeper with each number you count.

(Pause)

Gently focus back on the counting as each number brings you closer and closer to sleep.

(Pause)

Calm. Relaxed.

Peaceful and relaxed.

Continue to count down, all the way down, down to zero...

Down to sleep.

Get Back to Sleep

Getting back to sleep can be difficult, especially for those who experience insomnia. Relaxation is how to sleep after waking up by relaxing your mind and body again. This relaxation script will help you to calm your thoughts and return your body to a sleepy, restful state.

 Lie down, and get comfortable, adjusting your position as needed so you can fall asleep.

You will get back to sleep once your mind and body relax...and even if all you do is relax without sleeping, you will be rested and refreshed afterward.

Breathe deeply in...and slowly out...

Breathe in...and slowly breathe out...

Take slow, calm breaths.

Feel your breathing relax you. There is nothing you need to do right now, besides breathe calmly. Just drift...relaxing. Feel yourself becoming sleepy...ever so slowly getting sleepier.

(Pause)

See how slowly you can release the next breath you take. Breathe in deeply...and now breathe out slowly...very slowly...prolonging this breath out...relaxing...When you finish breathing out, breathe in naturally...and then breathe out again slowly.

Just keep breathing now, letting each breath occur naturally, without effort, at whatever pace is comfortable for you. Feel your breathing becoming calm...slow...easy.

(Pause)

Allow your body to relax. Feel your shoulders relaxing, the muscles releasing their hold.

Your legs are still...and they are starting to feel heavy. Your feet are very warm...feel the warmth spreading as your legs become warmer as well.

Your arms are getting heavier. Feel yourself sinking into the surface you are lying on. Sinking deeper...deeper...your whole body is feeling very heavy.

Feel the warmth in your hands, growing warmer and warmer... spreading up to your arms. Your hands and arms are very heavy.

Blink your eyes a few times, if you want to. Notice that your eyelids are feeling heavy. They are getting heavier and heavier, and it feels so good to close your eyes...to rest your eyes...allowing your eyes to remain closed...relaxed.

Notice a feeling of coolness in your forehead. Calm, cool, and relaxed. Smooth, free from tension.

Imagine that the tension in your body is flowing out through your fingers and your toes. Draining away...with each breath you can feel the tension leaving right out your finger tips and right out your toes. Feel the tension leaving your body, draining away.

(Pause)

Let you mind drift now for a moment, just relaxing. Not needing to focus, or think...just drifting, as the tension continues to drain away and your body relaxes.

(Pause)

You can actually feel the tension as it flows to your hands and feet, and away. Leaving only a feeling of relaxation. Notice this feeling that is left after the tension is gone. A soft, warm, relaxed feeling.

Your body is so heavy and relaxed. Sinking down...down...deeper and deeper. Back to sleep.

(Pause)

Now focus your mind for a moment, as you count each breath.

Breathe in...one...out...one...

In...two...out...two...

...Three...

...Four...

...Five...

Keep counting now on your own, focusing just on the numbers as I talk. Allow these words to pass through your mind, without needing to focus on any of them. Just concentrating on the numbers. If you lose count, begin again at one. Just keep counting, focusing only on the numbers.

Your body is so relaxed. So heavy. Back to sleep.

Thoughts drifting...but turning back to the numbers, with effort... because you are so tired.

Feeling very sleepy...hard to focus...your mind is drifting away...drifting back to sleep...falling asleep...

Bringing your consciousness back to the counting, focusing on the numbers...all other thoughts just drifting away...pleasantly drifting.

Your mind...thoughts...relaxed...sleepy...away...back to sleep...

Counting again, counting with each breath...relaxation growing with each number...

Sleepy and calm...

Not able to focus any longer...the numbers are blending together... losing count...too sleepy to count...

Start counting again at one, counting with each breath...two...three... four...five...

Keep counting, deeply relaxed. Drifting deeper...hardly able to focus...

May focus on the numbers...or the words...sleepy...

It's okay to just relax now...no need to count...or to focus...just allowing the sleep to overtake you.

Letting your mind drift off...drifting...drifting back to sleep...

It feels so good to surrender to the heaviness of sleep...

(Pause)

Imagine a beautiful place in your mind. A place of peace and serenity... so serene...so calm...a place that makes you happy. A place that is safe... quiet...

Your body is like a feather now, floating down gently toward this peaceful land of sleep. Feel your body drifting back and forth, down and down, fluttering through the air softly.

Will soon be coming to rest in this peaceful place. Softly resting, sinking...a peaceful, pleasant place. So sleepy...drifting down...down...

Sinking down into sleep...back to sleep...so deeply asleep and heavy...

Pleasant...calm...dreaming...

Coming to rest on a soft surface...softly sinking into comfort and sleep.

There are no more words you need to focus on...

Enjoy the relaxation now...and allow yourself to drift off into pleasant, deep sleep.

Autogenic Relaxation Scripts

Autogenic Relaxation

"Autogenics" is a relaxation technique that allows you to relax each part of your body by imagining that it is warm and heavy.

Begin reading the relaxation script here:

Find a comfortable position to sit or lie down. Autogenic relaxation is an effective relaxation technique that will allow you to relax your body and calm your mind.

Begin by breathing deeply, drawing air in...deep into your lungs...and releasing the breath slowly...

Breathe in...2...3...4...hold...2...3...exhale...2...3...4...5...

Again...2...3...4...pause...2...3...breathe out...2...3...4...5...

Continue taking slow, regular breaths.

Now turn your attention to your right hand. Feel the skin on the palm of your right hand becoming warm and relaxed. Feel the warmth in each finger...and on your palm...spreading to the back of your hand...to your wrist...

Feel your right arm becoming warm...

Your right arm is starting to feel very heavy...very heavy, and very relaxed.

Your right arm is warm, heavy, and relaxed.

Now focus on your left hand. Picture placing your left hand into soothing, warm water. Feel the warmth relaxing your hand completely. Allow your wrist to enter the warm, calming water...and relax.

Your arm is becoming heavy. Allow your left arm to sink into the warm water. Your left arm feels warm, heavy, and relaxed.

Now turn your attention to your legs. Feel your legs becoming warm. Feel the warmth spreading all the way from your feet...to your ankles... lower legs...knees...and hips. Feel your legs becoming heavy...very heavy, and very relaxed.

Your legs are warm...heavy...and relaxed...

Imagine a warm breeze blowing across your face...feel your face and head relaxing...your eyelids are very heavy...

Picture the sun shining down on you...warming the front of your body...allow your chest and stomach to relax in this warmth...feel the sun shining...warming your skin...relaxing your body...as your body is filled with heavy, warm, pleasant relaxation.

Now imagine sitting with your back to a pleasant campfire. Feel the warmth of the fire on your back. Feel your back warming and relaxing... the warmth spreads all the way from your neck...to your shoulders... your upper back...middle and lower back...feel your body relaxing as it becomes warm and calm...

Feel the heaviness in your entire body...your body is warm...heavy...and relaxed...

Enjoy this calm, relaxed feeling.

Notice your smooth, even breathing...relaxed and deep...drawing you even deeper into relaxation...

Your body feels very heavy...warm...and relaxed...

Enjoy the relaxation for a few more moments...

(Pause)

Now slowly begin to bring your attention back to the present...keeping your eyes closed...notice the room around you...notice the surface that you are lying or sitting on...hear the sounds in your environment...

Gently start to reawaken your body...wiggle your fingers and toes... move your arms and legs a little...stretch if you like...

When you are ready, open your eyes...and become fully alert.

Autogenics

Autogenics involves imagining that your limbs are warm and heavy, your heart rate is slow and steady, and your forehead is cool. This process will induce the relaxation response.

Begin reading the script here:

Begin by finding a comfortable position, seated or lying down.

Focus completely on your breathing. Let all other thoughts go.

Breathe in...2...3...4...hold...2...3...exhale...2...3...4...5...

Breathe in...2...3...4...hold...2...3...exhale...2...3...4...5...

Breathe in...2...3...4...hold...2...3...exhale...2...3...4...5...

Focus on just your breathing. There is nothing else you need to be doing at this moment. Nowhere else you need to be. Allow your worries to be released as you simply focus on the present. Breathe.

Breathe in...2...3...4...hold...2...3...exhale...2...3...4...5...

Breathe in...2...3...4...hold...2...3...exhale...2...3...4...5...

Breathe in...2...3...4...hold...2...3...exhale...2...3...4...5...

Keep breathing slowly and calmly.

(Pause)

Continue the autogenics process by turning your attention to your right hand. Imagine your right hand becoming warm. Starting at the tips of your thumb and fingers, the feeling of warmth spreads to your palm...to the back of your hand...to your wrist...

Your right hand is very warm...very heavy...relaxed.

Focus now on your left hand. Feel the feeling of warmth in your left hand...in your thumb and fingers...your palm...the back of your hand...your wrist...

Your left hand is warm, heavy, and relaxed.

Notice your right arm becoming heavy and warm. Relaxing into warmth and heaviness...your forearm...elbow...upper arm...

Your whole right arm is warm...very warm and heavy...the feeling of heaviness is very comfortable and relaxing...

Now turn your attention to your left arm. Feel your left arm warming, relaxing...Your left arm feels warm and heavy. Feel your left forearm...elbow...upper arm relaxing...warming...your entire left arm is heavy and warm...very relaxed.

Turn your attention now to your feet. Notice the feeling of warmth spreading from your right toes...to your right foot...the bottom of your foot...the top of your foot...your ankle...your right foot feels very heavy...warmer...heavier...relaxed.

Feel the warmth beginning in the toes of your left foot. Your left foot is becoming warm...from the bottom of your left foot...to the top...to your ankle...your left foot is warm...heavy...relaxing...

Both of your feet are pleasantly warm...a relaxed feeling of heaviness...warmth...and relaxation...

Feel the relaxation moving...growing...your right lower leg becomes warm...your knee...your right upper leg...your right leg is heavy and warm...

Feel your left lower leg warming and relaxing...your knee...upper leg...your left leg is warm and heavy...

Both of your legs are completely relaxed...

Repeat the following relaxing statements in your mind, imagining each one:

My right arm is warm.

My left arm is warm.

My right arm is heavy.

My left arm is heavy.

My right arm is warm and heavy.

My left arm is warm and heavy.

Both arms are warm and heavy.

My right leg is warm.

My right leg is heavy.

My left leg is warm.

My left leg is heavy.

Both legs are warm and heavy.

My arms and legs are warm.

My arms and legs are heavy.

My arms and legs are very warm and very heavy.

My heart rate is slow and regular.

My heart beat is slowing comfortably.

My forehead is cool.

My arms and legs are warm and heavy.

My heart beat is slow and steady.

My forehead is cool.

My arms and legs are very warm...relaxed...

My arms and legs are so heavy and relaxed...

My heartbeat is steady...slow...relaxed ...

My forehead is smooth and cool...

I am relaxed...

I am relaxed...

(Pause)

I am relaxed...

(Pause)

So warm...heavy...

Peaceful and serene...

Relaxed...

Now it is time to reawaken your body from this autogenics session. Feel your mind becoming more alert.

Wiggle your fingers. Feel your hands and arms reawakening.

Wiggle your toes.

Take a deep breath in as you stretch your arms, reaching high above your head. Exhale and lower your arms.

Open your eyes, and sit quietly for a moment as you become fully alert.

When you have returned to your usual level of wakefulness, your autogenics session is complete.

Warm Autogenic Relaxation Script

This warm autogenic relaxation script will guide you to imagine that each part of your body is warming and relaxing. Relax your whole body with a pleasant feeling of warmth.

Begin reading the script here:

To begin, find a comfortable position, either sitting or lying down.

Take a moment to settle in, just noticing how your body feels. Observe the state of your body, without trying to change anything, mentally scanning your body for areas of tension.

Take a deep breath in, and out.

Breathe in...and out.

Continue to take slow, regular breaths. Imagine that the areas of tension in your body relax a little each time you exhale.

Now let's begin the autogenic relaxation process.

Starting with your feet, begin to relax your body. Notice that your feet are becoming warm and relaxed. Focus on your left foot, feeling the bottom of your left foot becoming warmer. Feel your toes warming... and the top of your foot. Your entire left foot is warm.

Notice now your right foot. Feel the sole of your right foot warming and relaxing...the toes of your right foot are also becoming warm...and the top of your foot. Your whole right foot is warm.

A feeling of warmth and heaviness feels very pleasant. Feel the warmth in your feet increasing...continuing up to your ankles...and your lower legs.

At the same time as the warmth is growing in your feet and legs, turn your attention to your hands. Notice your right hand warming. Feel the warmth in each finger...starting at your finger tips...the warmth spreads to your fingers and your thumb, continuing to the palm of your right hand...Feel the back of your right hand warming as well.

Notice your left hand becoming warm...from the tip of each finger and your thumb...until your fingers and thumb are warm. Feel the warmth spread to the palm of your left hand...and the back of your hand. Your left hand is completely warm.

Feel the warmth in your hands increasing. Your hands are very warm... heavy...and relaxed.

The warmth continues to your wrists...and lower arms.

This pleasant feeling of warmth continues to your elbows...upper arms...your shoulders. Your arms and hands are very warm...very warm and heavy...relaxed.

Turn your attention again to your feet and legs. Notice the warmth in your feet and lower legs...continuing to your knees...upper legs...hips. Your legs are warm and heavy...pleasantly relaxed.

Feel the core of your body relaxing. A feeling of warmth begins in the center of your body, near your stomach. Feel the warmth growing...to your chest...all the way up to your neck. The front of your body, all the way from your hips to your neck, is warm, heavy, and relaxed.

Focus on the small of your back. Feel this area warming and relaxing. Allow the warmth to continue from your lower back, to your middle back, and upper back. Your back is warm...very relaxed.

Concentrate on your neck...feeling how warm and relaxed your neck has become.

Feel the relaxation in your entire body...a feeling of warmth and heaviness...very pleasant and relaxed.

Take a few moments now to just relax...enjoying the relaxation...calm... peaceful...relaxed...

(Pause)

Relax for a few moments longer, luxuriating in the feelings of calm and warmth.

(Pause)

When you are ready to finish your relaxation session, give yourself a few moments to wake up your body and mind. Move your fingers and toes, arms and legs. Stretch a little to wake up sleepy muscles.

Take a deep, refreshing breath in...and exhale, reawakening. One more deep breath in...and out.

When you have returned to your usual level of alertness, the autogenic relaxation session is complete. You can return to your day, feeling calm, relaxed, and refreshed.

Sensory Relaxation Scripts

Sensory Relaxation

This sensory relaxation script will guide you to imagine a variety of sensations to help focus the mind and promote relaxation. This journey through the senses will include sight, sound, smell, taste, touch and movement.

To begin the sensory relaxation process, imagine that you are at the top of a stairway. At the bottom of the stairway is a state of peace, calm, and relaxation. Notice how you are feeling right now, at the top of the stairway.

Begin to descend the stairway, going down toward relaxation...down and down to a state of calm and relaxation.

Picture yourself going slowly down the stairway, one step at a time. It is a comfortable, safe descent to a place of relaxation. Move down step by step, at your own pace, becoming more and more relaxed with each step.

You might even become a bit sleepy as you get closer and closer to relaxation. That's okay. Allow your mind to drift and your body to relax, heavy and comfortable.

Moving down the stairway, down, down...almost to the bottom now... when you reach the bottom you will be pleasantly relaxed.

(Pause)

Now that you are experiencing a feeling of relaxation, create a mental picture in your mind of these relaxing visual images.

Imagine looking at an entire field of flowers from a great distance. See the flowers growing all the way to the horizon, as far as you can see. Focus in closer and closer until you are able to focus on several blossoms at arm's length.

Now imagine looking at one beautiful flower. See the color of the flower in your mind. See the petals, the leaves, the stem. Imagine looking at the flower from very close up. See the minute details of the flower including any texture in the petals, drops of water, grains of pollen.

Create a new visual image in your mind now...imagine that you are looking at a piece of crystal. As the light shines on the crystal, a rainbow of colors appears.

The crystal itself is transparent, but becomes bathed in a variety of colors as light is transformed on its surfaces and within the crystal. See the shining colors...moving...ever changing...flowing...see the surfaces of the crystal and the light shining upon them and reflecting off of them. Are the surfaces smooth or rough? Rounded? Sharp?

Imagine this beautiful piece of crystal. Picture turning and moving the crystal to see the light play upon the crystal and radiate from it. Can you see through the crystal? What does that look like? Imagine looking at the colors, textures, and shape of the crystal.

Let's move on now to one of the other senses: hearing.

Can you imagine the sound of waves? Hear in your mind the sound of waves washing to shore.

What about the sounds of a park on a sunny day? You might hear birds singing, children playing, people talking, dogs barking, a splashing fountain...imagine the sounds of the breeze blowing at the park...the sounds of a game of catch...laughter...the rhythmic thud of a ball as it is caught in a glove, thrown, and caught in a glove again...

What other sounds might you hear at the park?

Now imagine a different sound. The sound of rain on a roof. Imagine the sound of the rain as each drop lands. You may hear the sound of a gentle rain, a few scattered drops. Or you may hear a harder rain, the constant tap tap tap of many drops landing together. Hear the sound of the rain.

Now let's imagine the sense of smell.

Can you imagine the scent of baking cookies?

Imagine the smell of baking bread.

The smell of a pine forest. Smell the pine trees...the soil...the smell of the outdoors.

Imagine the smell of a rose. Imagine the smell of the rose so clearly, it is as if there is a rose right in front of you, and you have brought it close to your nose to inhale its sweet scent.

Now, move on to imagine the sense of taste.

Imagine placing a slice of lemon against your tongue...imagine the sour taste of the lemon if you were to bite into the slice.

Now imagine the taste of something sweet—a candy, a cookie.

Think of a food that you like...now imagine taking a bite of this food. Taste the food.

Let's imagine now the sense of touch.

Picture an animal that you like—maybe a friendly dog, cat, or rabbit—with very soft fur. Imagine stroking the animal...feel the soft fur on the palm of your hand. Imagine moving your hand along the sleek fur.

Imagine now a tub of warm water that is big enough to place your feet in. Imagine placing your bare feet into the tub of water. The water is pleasantly hot. Feel the warm water on your feet, all the way up to your ankles.

Think of holding an object in your hands that is very soft...perhaps a sponge. Imagine squeezing the sponge.

Now think of an object that is hard...like a stone. Imagine holding a hard, smooth, cool stone in your hands.

Think of touching something rough, like the bark of a tree. Imagine moving your hand along the tree bark and feeling the details of the rough surface.

Imagine wrapping up in a heavy blanket. Feel the blanket wrapped tightly around you...providing firm but gentle pressure all over your body. Very comfortable and heavy.

Let's move on to the last sensation now, the sensation of movement.

Imagine lying in a hammock that is gently swaying. Feel the slight movement from left...to right...left...to right...calming and repetitive movement.

Can you imagine the feeling of being on a roller coaster? Imagine the feeling of accelerating forward, going up an incline...slowing as you reach the top, going up the last bit, leveling off...and rushing over the other side, accelerating very fast down, down, down...reaching the bottom, and rushing up the next hill and around a curve...fast turns... feel the movement of a roller coaster ride.

Now imagine a different movement...moving your body. Imagine running...taking great strides as you almost fly along, running quickly, smoothly, and easily...feel the movement of your muscles, your arms and legs...feel each step...

Lastly, imagine how it would feel if you were able to fly. Imagine moving through the air, feel the movement as you glide, turn, move up, down...fly through the sky.

This brief journey through the senses has allowed you to experience sensory relaxation. Now it is time to return to the present...to get back in touch with your environment.

Imagine a staircase once again. You are at the bottom of the staircase right now. At the top of the staircase is a state of alertness, awareness, and calm. When you reach the top of the staircase, you will be fully awake and alert, ready to complete your usual daily activities, and maintaining a feeling of calm.

Proceed up the staircase, moving higher, higher, higher...reaching the middle of the staircase, becoming more and more alert...nearing the top...a few more steps...take the last few steps up to the top of the staircase, reaching the top.

Take a deep breath...and exhale...feeling calm and alert.

Emotional Awareness Relaxation

This emotional awareness relaxation is a sensory relaxation process that can allow you to become more aware of feelings based on the sensory experience of an emotion. This script is especially relevant for survivors of trauma, but can also be effective for anyone who wants to better understand emotions.

By familiarizing yourself with the sensory experience of emotions, you can become skilled at recognizing what it is you are feeling in a given moment, and address both positive and negative emotions you experience in daily life.

 The word "feeling" is used to refer to emotions and to sensations. This is because emotions and sensations are closely linked. The connection between the mind and body causes emotional responses to be reflected in the physical body.

The book "*The Body Remembers: The Psychophysiology of Trauma and Trauma Treatment,*" by Babette Rothschild, discusses emotions and the body. This book provides more information about emotions as a physical body experience.[12]

Begin reading the script here:

In this emotional awareness relaxation script, I'll guide you to focus on feelings, one at a time, and notice the effect of each emotion on your body. As you do this exercise, be aware that some of the feelings are unpleasant, but this discomfort can be important and helpful. You will spend about half a minute with each feeling.

It is important to be aware that some parts of this emotional awareness relaxation script will be uncomfortable. Before beginning the relaxation exercise, I'll guide you to create a safety zone in your mind. If any aspects of this exercise become too uncomfortable, you can mentally go

---

[12] Rothschild, B. (2000). *The Body Remembers: The Psychophysiology of Trauma and Trauma Treatment*, P 56 - 64. W.W. Norton & Company, Ltd. New York, NY.

to the safety zone for a break. Make sure to keep yourself safe and respect your limits when doing this or any other relaxation exercise.

Let's begin. Sit or lie down, and make yourself comfortable.

Begin to relax your body by focusing for the next few moments on breathing. Take a deep breath in...and breathe out.

In...and out.

Breathe in again, and as you exhale, release the tension in your body.

Breathe in...and exhale, releasing tension.

Continue breathing slowly, allowing your breaths to relax you.

Create a picture in your mind of a place of safety. Picture a place where you felt safe as a child, or a place you feel safe now. Where would you go when you needed a break? Did you have a favorite room, or chair, or place outdoors? Think of a place were you have felt safe before, and imagine this place in your mind. Picture all the details of the safe place.

(Pause)

Now that you have the safe place fixed in your mind, this image can serve as your safety zone. Notice how you are feeling right now. Feel the feeling of being safe. How does it feel to be safe? How does your stomach feel when you feel safe? How about your muscles? Your face? Where in your body do you feel this feeling of safety?

Notice your body while you have this feeling right now. If you need a break during this script, you can mentally return to this place by imagining your safety zone. Do so whenever you need to.

An emotion may be experienced in one place in your body, or several. When you experience each of the feelings I mention, notice where in your body you are feeling something. Also notice what you are feeling.

For example, you may experience feelings of heaviness, tightness, tingling, pain, comfort, lightness, warmth or fluttering.

Notice your body as a whole and the individual parts of your body. You may notice changes in muscle tension (clenched jaw or relaxed jaw, tight or loose fists, etc). You may notice changes in the way your face, stomach, head, chest, throat, or other areas feel.

With each emotion I mention, I will guide you to experience the associated physical sensations. Each time, just notice how your body is feeling, what it feels like, and where the sensations are located. Remember that if you need a break at any time, you can mentally return to your safety zone.

 Now let's begin the sensory process of experiencing emotions and getting in touch with feelings.

Imagine a feeling of happiness. Think of a time when you felt happy, and allow yourself to experience some of this feeling again now. What does "happy" feel like in your body? Create these sensations now. Where in your body is the feeling of happiness located? Experience the physical sensations of happiness for a few moments.

(Pause)

Now imagine the feeling of anger. Think of a time when you were feeling angry, and allow yourself to experience some of this feeling again now. What does "anger" feel like in your body? Where in your body is the feeling of anger located? Experience the physical sensations of anger for a few moments.

(Pause)

Imagine the feeling of pride. Think of a time when you were feeling proud, and allow yourself to experience some of this feeling again now. What does "pride" feel like in your body? Where in your body is the feeling of pride located? Experience the physical sensations of pride for a few moments.

(Pause)

Now imagine the feeling of sadness. Think of a time when you were feeling sad, and allow yourself to experience some of this feeling again now. What does "sad" feel like in your body? Where in your body is the feeling of sadness located? Experience the physical sensations of sadness for a few moments.

(Pause)

Now imagine the feeling of excitement. Think of a time when you were feeling excited, and allow yourself to experience some of this feeling again now. What does "excited" feel like in your body? Where in your body is the feeling of excitement located? Experience the physical sensations of excitement for a few moments.

(Pause)

Now imagine the feeling of guilt. Think of a time when you were feeling guilty, and allow yourself to experience some of this feeling again now. What does "guilt" feel like in your body? Where in your body is the feeling of guilt located? Experience the physical sensations of guilt for a few moments.

(Pause)

Imagine the feeling of interest. Think of a time when you were feeling interested, and allow yourself to experience some of this feeling again now. What does "interested" feel like in your body? Where in your body is the feeling of interest located? Experience the physical sensations of interest for a few moments.

(Pause)

 Now imagine the feeling of embarrassment. Think of a time when you were feeling embarrassed, and allow yourself to experience some of this feeling again now. What does "embarrassment" feel like in your body? Where in your body is the feeling of embarrassment located? Experience the physical sensations of embarrassment for a few moments.

(Pause)

Imagine the feeling of amusement. Think of a time when you were feeling amused, and allow yourself to experience some of this feeling again now. What does "amusement" feel like in your body? Where in your body is the feeling of amusement located? Experience the physical sensations of amusement for a few moments.

(Pause)

Now imagine the feeling of joy. Think of a time when you were feeling joyful, and allow yourself to experience some of this feeling again now. What does "joyful" feel like in your body? Where in your body is the feeling of joy located? Experience the physical sensations of joy for a few moments.

(Pause)

You have imagined several feelings. Now just relax, and allow the feelings that arise for you to be present for a moment. Notice how you are feeling right now, without trying to encourage or discourage any particular emotions. Just be. Let yourself feel whatever it is that comes up for you.

Notice how your body feels. Where in your body are you feeling something? What does this tell you about the emotions you are experiencing?

Does your body feel right now the way it did when you imagined a particular emotion a few moments ago? If so, which one?

Can you identify the feeling or feelings you have right now? Is there a name for any of the emotions you are experiencing in this moment? Just notice, observing the state of your body and allowing your body to speak to you.

(Pause)

Notice that all of the emotions, both positive and negative, can serve a useful purpose. It is okay to feel. It is normal and natural to have emotions. When you are in tune with your body, you can allow your body to speak to you, and find out what your body is telling you. Your body will let you know which situations are positive, and which ones you may want to change.

You will experience both positive and negative feelings. From time to time, you can deliberately help yourself feel good by imagining a positive emotion and the physical feelings that accompany it.

Let's do that right now. Imagine again the feeling of happiness. Where in your body is this feeling located? You can experience this feeling now. Feel the sensations in your body that accompany happiness. Allow the sensations to build, and grow...feeling a positive sensation of happiness.

Just be with this feeling for a few moments. Let the sensory relaxation process evoke the physical and emotional feeling of happiness.

(Pause)

When you are ready to conclude this process, keep with you the feeling of happiness and a feeling of calm.

Return your awareness to the present, noticing the environment around you.

When you are fully awake and alert, you can return to your usual activities, feeling happy and calm.

Relaxation Scripts for Children

Relaxation for Children

Relaxation for children that guides children or adults to relax using simple breathing and progressive relaxation techniques. This script is intended to be used with the guidance of an adult.

This script relaxation for children is a short script intended for those who are new in learning relaxation or for those who enjoy brief and simple relaxation techniques, and can be used as a quick method of relaxation for children or adults.

Begin reading the script here:

Get ready to relax. You can sit in a chair or lie down on a bed.

Close your eyes, and take a deep breath in...now breathe out.

Breathe in...and breathe out.

Keep breathing slowly like this. Feel how it relaxes you to breathe deeply.

Now squeeze your hands closed into fists. Pretend that you are squeezing a ball in each hand...gripping tighter...squeeze even tighter... right now, your muscles are tense.

And now relax. Let your hands go limp. Now your hands feel relaxed. See how relaxed your hands feel. See how tense feels different from relaxed. Relaxation is a way to make your whole body feel relaxed like your hands are now.

One way to relax your body is by breathing deeply. Imagine that your body is like a balloon. When you breathe in, feel your chest and sides expanding, like a balloon filling with air. When you breathe out, imagine your body is like a balloon shrinking with the air being let out.

Breathe in like a balloon being blown up. Now breathe out, like the air is being let out of a balloon. Let the air out by blowing the air through your mouth.

Breathe in through your nose, imagining your body expanding like a balloon...and now imagine letting the end of the balloon go, and the air rushing out as you breathe out through your mouth.

As you breathe in this time, raise your arms above your head. When you breathe out, lower your arms.

Breathe in. Reach your hands above your head, stretching high up... stretching...and now lower your arms to your sides and relax. Breathe out.

Raise your arms and breathe in...lower your arms and breathe out...

Raise your arms and breathe in...lower your arms and breathe out...

Now relax and keep your arms at your sides, while you continue breathing slowly and deeply.

Remember the difference between tense and relaxed. Tighten your leg muscles to make both of your legs tense. Squeeze tighter...tighter...and now relax.

Let your legs become very relaxed. Each leg is as floppy as a piece of string.

Your legs feel heavy. The muscles are loose.

Now tense your arms. Make the muscles very tight and tense. Tighter...and now relax. Your arms are relaxed, limp and loose as pieces of string.

See how it feels to be relaxed. Your legs and arms are relaxed.

Now let your whole body become relaxed. See how relaxed you can make your body...loosening every muscle...no tension at all...

Your body feels heavy and relaxed.

Relax even more by noticing your breathing again. See how calm your breathing is.

In...and out...

In...and out...

Keep breathing and simply relax. There is nothing you need to do right now except relax quietly.

(Pause)

See how calm and relaxed you feel. It feels good to relax.

Your relaxation time is finished now, and it is time to return to your usual activities. Keep your eyes closed for a little longer while you wake up your body and your mind by wiggling your fingers and toes... moving your arms and legs...

Sit still now for a moment, and open your eyes to look around the room.

When you are ready, get up and return to your usual activities, feeling awake, but still feeling relaxed and calm.

Breathing Relaxation for Children

This breathing relaxation for children is for anyone who is learning to relax. Both children and adults can use this breathing relaxation exercise as an easy relaxation technique.

Begin reading the script here:

Do you ever feel stressed, or worried, or tense? Relaxation lets you feel calm and peaceful. You can learn to feel calm by using breathing for relaxation. Taking deep breaths helps your body get the air it needs, and it can help you to calm down when you need to. It feels good to relax.

Begin the breathing relaxation for children.

Let's relax right now. First, let your body relax a bit. Reach up, high above your head, stretching your arms...stretching your body very tall. Now let your arms relax. Place them at your sides, loosely.

Do the same thing again, but this time, breathe in as you reach up. Stretch...and now breathe out as you relax and place your arms at your sides.

One more stretch, arms up, breathing in...and relax, arms down, breathing out.

Just sit now, letting your arms rest at your sides.

See how your breathing can relax you by taking slow, deep breaths. Breathe in...hold your breath...and now breathe out, slowly. Breathe in...and out.

Keep breathing deeply and slowly.

Continue the breathing relaxation for children.

Place one hand on your chest and one hand on your stomach. Feel both of your hands moving up and out as you breathe in...and down as you breathe out. Feel your hands moving with your chest and stomach, gently moving in and out with each breath.

(Pause)

Now rest your hands at your sides as you notice the ways you can breathe. Continue the breathing relaxation for children.

Imagine that there is a candle in front of you. You can even hold up one finger in front of your mouth and pretend it is a candle, if you like. As you breathe out, blow the air out through your mouth very slowly. Feel the air on your finger. Imagine that you are blowing enough air to make the flame of the candle flicker, but not enough to blow it out. You will need to blow very softly.

When you breathe in, imagine that the flame of the candle flickers and leans toward you. As you breathe out, the flame flickers and leans away.

Imagine the flame of the candle moving in and out with each breath you take. Continue the breathing relaxation for children.

(Pause)

Another way your breathing can relax you is to breathe like different animals. Do you know how a dog pants? Breathe in...and now as you breathe out, pant, ha ha ha ha ha ha ha. Breathe in...pant, ha ha ha ha ha. Breathe in...pant.

Imagine that you are like a cat purring. Breathe in...and as you breathe out, purr. Breathe in...purr. Breathe in...purr.

Now as you breathe, you can sigh, and relax. Breathe in...and sigh as you breathe out. Breathe in...sigh. Breathe in...sigh.

Just relax now for a moment, feeling your body relax. Your arms and legs are very loose and relaxed. Continue the breathing relaxation for children.

Now you can imagine that your body is like a balloon filling up as you breathe in, and emptying as you breathe out. Let your ribs expand out to the sides, like a balloon, expanding...and then let the air out, like a balloon that is emptying. The balloon expands...and then the air goes out.

You can even imagine that you are blowing up a balloon. Imagine that you breathe air into your lungs, and then when you breathe out through your mouth, imagine that you are blowing up a balloon. Each breath you blow out makes the balloon get even bigger. Imagine filling the balloon as it gets bigger and bigger with each breath out. Breathe in...and then blow up the balloon even more. Bigger...bigger...bigger.

Imagine letting go of the balloon, so it flies around the room as the air escapes. Feel your body relaxing just like a limp, empty balloon. Continue the breathing relaxation for children.

And now, see how slowly you can breathe out. First breathe in...and now breathe out very slowly...out...out...out. When you can't breathe out any more air, breathe in again, and then very slowly breathe out.

For the next few moments, just relax, resting. It feels good to relax. Enjoy this calm feeling.

(Pause)

Now you are finished this breathing relaxation for children. Stretch your muscles if you want to, and let your body wake up. When you are totally awake, you can get back to the rest of your day.

Relaxation to Stop Being Afraid of the Dark

This relaxation script is for children or adults who are afraid of the dark. It begins with visualization and calming phrases to bring comfort and relaxation, and ends with passive progressive muscle relaxation. Listen to this relaxation script before bed to fall asleep comfortably.

Begin reading the script here:

Many people of all ages are afraid of the dark...but there is nothing to fear about darkness.

If you need to turn on the light for a few seconds, do that now. Look around the room...see the things that are here. Now turn the lights out, and look around. See how everything looks different in the dark...but really it is all still the same.

Get into bed and get comfortable...settling in beneath the blankets. Close your eyes, and start to relax. You are safe right now.

It's okay to be scared...but there is nothing to be afraid of. You don't need to be afraid of the dark anymore. Any time you start to feel afraid, just remember looking around the room a minute ago with the lights on, and then with the lights off. You know that everything looks different when it's dark, but you are still in the same, safe place as before.

People feel afraid of the dark because they imagine scary things. When you imagine scary things, you feel scared.

You can feel less afraid by thinking about something else. Use your imagination to feel good instead of scared.

First, let's focus on breathing. Think just about your breathing. Take a big breath in...and breathe out.

Take another breath in...and out.

Keep breathing slowly...and deeply...and feel yourself starting to relax. It feels good to breathe slowly and deeply.

Now, let's focus on an imaginary place...a happy, safe, peaceful place.

Imagine a place where you are safe and happy. You might picture a castle, meadow, beach, mountain...imagine a nice place where you feel happy, calm, and relaxed.

Imagine all the details of this place...you feel so safe and relaxed in this nice place. Create a picture in your mind of being outdoors at your peaceful place. It is a bright, sunny day...warm and pleasant.

Feel the sun shining down on you...so warm...so comforting. See the blue sky above, and the soft, white clouds drifting by.

It is so peaceful here...you feel so relaxed...so calm...

You can visit this place in your imagination any time you want to feel relaxed and safe.

I would like to repeat some phrases about feeling calm and safe in the dark. If you start to feel afraid, just imagine your happy, peaceful place again. Imagine this place whenever you need to while I talk.

There is nothing to fear in the dark. You don't need to be afraid of the dark.

You are safe here.

Remember that the room you are in is just the same as it was when the light was on.

You can feel calm and happy in the dark.

Night time is the time to sleep...the darkness is nice because it helps you sleep so you can feel awake and rested in the morning.

Being in the dark is peaceful.

You can close your eyes and imagine being anywhere you want to be. See how easy it is to imagine when you're in the dark...see how you can imagine happy things.

Notice that you are feeling less afraid than you were before. You are probably feeling quite relaxed because you know that there is nothing to worry about, and nothing to fear.

You were afraid of the dark before because you were imagining scary things. But now, you know how to use your imagination to think about happy things...peaceful places...pleasant thoughts.

It feels good to use your imagination like this, to think of happy things.

Whenever your mind plays tricks on you and you start thinking about scary things, and start feeling afraid, remember the peaceful place you imagined a few minutes ago. Remember how happy you felt as you imagined what it would be like to look up at the sky, with the sun shining down, and the clouds floating by.

See what a nice, happy picture your imagination can create? You have a wonderful imagination that you can use to picture all sorts of good and happy things.

Let's just relax now...becoming sleepy...

Imagine a peaceful place. Allow yourself to feel completely comfortable and happy in this place in your imagination.

Your eyelids feel heavy...and it feels good to just close your eyes... resting...relaxing...

You are feeling very calm...sleepy...happy...

(Pause)

When your body becomes relaxed, you can feel the relaxation. You will know that a part of you is relaxed because it feels a little different... maybe a bit warmer...or heavier...or more loose...maybe a bit tingly.

Focus on your hands...letting your hands relax, until they feel a little different. You can feel that relaxation. You can tell when your hands are relaxed by this nice feeling. Just let your hands go limp...good. Now your hands are relaxed.

Concentrate on your arms now, up to your elbows. Feel the relaxation in your arms. When your lower arms feel a little different, and are relaxed, think about your upper arms, all the way to your shoulders. Feel your arms relaxing...your arms feel very relaxed. They are heavy and loose...your hands and arms feel warm...warm, heavy, and relaxed.

Think about your feet now. Relax your feet. Your feet feel warm and heavy...and your legs feel relaxed...as limp as spaghetti...feel your legs relaxing. When you can feel the relaxation in your legs, move on to relax the rest of your body.

Let your tummy relax...it feels warm and comfortable.

Think about your back. Let your back relax all the way from the bottom of your back, up to your neck. Your back will feel a little different from how it did before...a nice, relaxed feeling.

Think about your chest...letting this part of you relax.

Think about your face...and your head...soon your face and head will feel relaxed.

Now think about your whole body...all the way from your feet to your head. If you notice anywhere that is not relaxed, just think about this area...and feel it relaxing. Your whole body is relaxed. You feel so good and so comfortable.

Just rest now...relax...feeling so sleepy...

Imagine a safe and peaceful place in your imagination...imagine a quiet, happy land of dreams...waiting for you when you fall asleep...such happy dreams you will have...

You are very sleepy...

Very relaxed...

It feels so nice to relax...falling asleep...

So safe and pleasant...

So comfortable...

Relaxed...

Sleepy...

Drifting off...

Drifting off to sleep...

Custom Relaxation Scripts

A wide variety of personalized relaxation scripts can be created using these parts. You can choose any induction, body, and conclusion, and combine these elements in order for a customized script.

The *induction* is the first part of the relaxation script, that leads the subject to begin to relax. The *body* is the main relaxation portion of the script; the focus or topic of the script. The *conclusion* is the ending. The script can finish by leading the subject to become alert and awake, or to fall asleep.

Note that anchoring[13] can be used after the relaxation segment and before the conclusion. I have included here two examples: Progressive Muscle Relaxation and Anchoring (body of a relaxation script), and Anchoring and Counting Back (conclusion). Anchoring can be used with any of the scripts, between the body and the conclusion.

---

[13] See the Anchoring Relaxation Script, page 212 for a description of how anchoring works.

Induction: Beginning of a Relaxation Script

Induction 1: Progressive Muscle Relaxation

Begin by finding a comfortable position, seated or lying down.

Take a deep breath in, and as you exhale, allow your body to begin to relax.

Breathe slowly and naturally.

Raise your shoulders toward your ears. Then, let your shoulders relax...dropping into a comfortable, loose position, and feel yourself sinking into the surface you are on.

Allow your jaw to drop slightly, letting the muscles of your face and jaw become loose and relaxed.

Wiggle your toes once or twice and feel your feet and legs relaxing.

Gently open and close your hands once...and again...and then relax your hands and arms.

Take a deep breath in, feeling the tension in your chest and stomach as you hold that breath...and allow your chest and stomach to relax as the breath escapes slowly.

Allow the muscles of your back to relax...from your neck...to your upper back...middle back...lower back...feeling your whole body relaxing.

Notice any areas of tension in your body, and relax those areas now.

Your body will continue to relax...deeper and deeper...loose...heavy... relaxed.

Induction 2: Breathing

As you begin this relaxation exercise, make yourself comfortable. Find a position that you can maintain for several minutes comfortably.

Begin to become aware of your breathing.

Notice each breath as it goes in...and out...

See how you can slow the rhythm of your breathing by counting. Breathe in to the count of four, hold for a count of three, and exhale to the count of five.

Breathe in...2...3...4...pause...2...3...breathe out...2...3...4...5...

Again...2...3...4...hold...2...3...exhale...2...3...4...5...

Breathe in...2...3...4...hold...2...3...exhale...2...3...4...5...

Breathe in...2...3...4...pause...2...3...breathe out...2...3...4...5...

Breathe in...2...3...4...hold...2...3...exhale...2...3...4...5...

Continue to breathe slowly, smoothly...relaxing more with each breath.

Feel yourself becoming more and more relaxed.

Induction 3: Awareness of Mind and Body

Get ready to relax your body and your mind. Settle into a comfortable position, and begin to turn your attention inward.

Notice how you are feeling right now...mentally...physically. Without trying to change anything, simply take note of how your body feels... and notice how you are feeling mentally.

Mentally scan your body now, looking for areas of tension. Where is your body the most tense?

Notice now where your body is most relaxed. See that these areas of relaxation are slowly getting larger...

Now turn your awareness to your breathing. Simply notice your breathing, without making any effort to change your breathing in any way.

Imagine breathing in relaxation...and breathing out tension.

Feel yourself becoming more relaxed with each breath.

Focus in on areas of tension in your body, and imagine directing your breath to these areas. Feel the breath in drawing in relaxation...and as you exhale, imagine the tension draining away from each area of tension. Allow your breathing to relax your body.

Feel your body and mind becoming relaxed...calm...peaceful.

Deeply relaxed and calm.

Induction 4: Stairway

To begin the relaxation process, imagine that you are at the top of a stairway. At the bottom of the stairway is a state of peace, calm, and relaxation.

Take note of how you are feeling right now, at the top of the stairway.

Imagine taking a step down the stairway...a single step closer to relaxation.

Further descend the stairway, going down toward relaxation...down... down...to a state of calm and relaxation.

Picture yourself going slowly down the stairway, one step at a time. It is a comfortable, safe descent to a place of relaxation. Move down step by step, at your own pace, becoming more and more relaxed with each step you take.

Take another step down...and another...more deeply relaxed with each step.

You might even become a bit sleepy as you get closer and closer to relaxation. That's okay. Allow your mind to drift and your body to relax, heavy and comfortable.

Moving down the stairway, down, down...almost to the bottom now... when you reach the bottom you will be pleasantly relaxed.

Take the last few steps down to the bottom of the stairway...

Reaching the bottom now...a state of calm and relaxation. You are now feeling peaceful and relaxed.

Induction 5: Counting Down

Get comfortable, preparing to relax. Find a position sitting or lying down, and start to relax your body.

Take a deep breath in...and breathe out...

In...and out...

Continue to breathe deeply, slowly, and comfortably.

I'll count down now, from ten...to one. As I say each number, you can become more relaxed.

Let's begin.

Ten...feeling your muscle start to relax...

Nine...your hands and feet are warming and relaxing...

Eight...your muscles are becoming loose and heavy...

Seven...notice your attention drifting...becoming more relaxed...

Six...relaxing even further now...peaceful...

Five...a tingly feeling of relaxation spreading through your body... pleasant and relaxed

Four...further relaxed and peaceful...

Three...free of tension...

Two...almost completely relaxed now...

One...you are now deeply relaxed.

Very deeply relaxed and comfortable.

Body: Middle of a Relaxation Script

Body 1: Meditation

Choose a focus word that you will concentrate your attention on. I'll use the word "calm" here as an example. As your thoughts wander, keep returning your attention to this word. It is normal and natural for your thoughts to wander. Just accept the thoughts as they come, and let the thoughts pass while you return your attention to your focus word.

As you inhale, imagine breathing in relaxation as you focus on the word, "calm."

As you exhale, repeat your focus word...calm.

Breathe in...calm...

Breathe out...calm...

Continue to breathe slowly and deeply. Repeat your focus word with each breath.

(Pause)

Return your attention again to your focus word, repeating with each breath...

Breathe in...calm...

Breathe out...calm...

Calm...

Calm...

Continue to focus on the word, "calm."

(Pause)

As your thoughts wander, return your attention to the word, "calm."
Repeating this word with each breath.

(Pause)

Breathe in...calm...

Breathe out...calm...

In...calm...

Out...calm...

Continue breathing slowly and deeply.

Body 2: Autogenics

Continue the relaxation process by turning your attention to your right hand. Imagine your right hand becoming warm. Starting at the tips of your thumb and fingers, the feeling of warmth spreads to your palm...to the back of your hand...to your wrist...

Your right hand is very warm...very heavy...relaxed.

Focus now on your left hand. Feel the feeling of warmth in your left hand...in your thumb and fingers...your palm...the back of your hand... your wrist...

Your left hand is warm, heavy, and relaxed.

Continue the autogenics session, enjoying the relaxation you are experiencing.

Notice your right arm becoming heavy and warm. Relaxing into warmth and heaviness...your forearm...elbow...upper arm...

Your whole right arm is warm...very warm and heavy...the feeling of heaviness is very comfortable and relaxing...

Now turn your attention to your left arm. Feel your left arm warming, relaxing...Your left arm feels warm and heavy. Feel your left forearm... elbow...upper arm relaxing...warming...your entire left arm is heavy and warm...very relaxed.

Turn your attention now to your feet. Notice the feeling of warmth spreading from your right toes...to your right foot...the bottom of your foot...the top of your foot...your ankle...Your right foot feels very heavy...warmer...heavier...relaxed.

Feel the warmth beginning in the toes of your left foot. Your left foot is becoming warm...from the bottom of your left foot...to the top...to your ankle...your left foot is warm...heavy...relaxing...

Both of your feet are pleasantly warm...a relaxed feeling of heaviness... warmth...and relaxation...

Feel the relaxation moving...growing...your right lower leg becomes warm...your knee...your right upper leg...your right leg is heavy and warm ...

Feel your left lower leg warming and relaxing...your knee...upper leg... your left leg is warm and heavy...

Both of your legs are completely relaxed...

Repeat the following relaxing statements in your mind, imagining each one:

My right arm is warm.

My left arm is warm.

My right arm is heavy.

My left arm is heavy.

My right arm is warm and heavy.

My left arm is warm and heavy.

Both arms are warm and heavy.

My right leg is warm.

My right leg is heavy.

My left leg is warm.

My left leg is heavy.

Both legs are warm and heavy.

My arms and legs are warm.

My arms and legs are heavy.

My arms and legs are very warm and very heavy.

My heart rate is slow and regular.

My heart beat is slowing comfortably.

My forehead is cool.

My arms and legs are warm and heavy.

My heart beat is slow and steady.

My forehead is cool.

My arms and legs are very warm...relaxed...

My arms and legs are so heavy and relaxed...

My heartbeat is steady...slow...relaxed...

My forehead is smooth and cool...

I am relaxed...

I am relaxed...

(Pause)

Body 3: Progressive Muscle Relaxation and Anchoring

Stretch the muscles of your face as you open your mouth wide and breathe in...yawn if you wish...stretch the muscles of your face...and let your face slacken gently as you breathe out...relax completely...let your lower jaw hang loosely below your upper jaw, your teeth not touching.

Scan your body for areas of tension as you take another deep breath in. Feel the tension in your body as you hold that breath. Now let the tension go as you let the breath go.

Point your toes, stretching your legs. Release the muscles of your legs and relax. Now bring your feet upward, toward your shins, stretching the back of your legs. Release the stretch, relaxing your legs completely.

Let your legs become limp...loose and relaxed...

Let your arms become relaxed and loose...

Notice how your body feels.

Feel the relaxation flowing through your body. Notice that you can become even more relaxed...wiggle your toes once or twice, and then allow your toes to be still and relaxed.

Feel the relaxation flowing...spreading...until your feet are relaxed as well.

Let the relaxation continue to your ankles. Feel how loose and relaxed your ankles feel.

Now allow the muscles of your lower legs to give up their hold. Feel the relaxation in your lower legs...calm...relaxed...heavy...relaxed...

Enjoy the feeling of relaxation as it continues to your knees...then your upper legs...feel your thighs relaxing and letting go...your legs feel very heavy...very heavy, and very relaxed...

Feel the relaxation flowing...allow your buttocks to relax...your pelvic area...and now your abdomen...feel the muscles becoming loose and relaxed...letting go of all the tension...relaxed and heavy...

Allow your lower back to relax...feel the relaxation there as the muscles of your lower back give up their hold...leaving nothing but relaxation...calm...peaceful...

Let the relaxation continue to flow throughout your body, spreading now to the muscles of your sides...feel your sides, abdomen, and chest gently moving in and out with each breath...each breath making you even more relaxed...

Allow the muscles of your sides to let go...feel the relaxation filling your core...relaxing your chest and stomach...your middle back...your upper back...

The relaxation continues to increase...pleasantly more and more relaxed...deeper and deeper...feel your shoulders relaxing...your upper arms...your elbows...

Feel your arms relaxing more and more...becoming heavier and heavier...let the relaxation continue...spreading to your lower arms...your wrists...and your hands...

Your arms become completely limp and relaxed...pleasant...relaxed...

Let the relaxation continue from your lower back...middle back...and upper back...to your neck...the back of your neck and the front of your neck...the back of your head...the top of your head...your chin...your face...your jaw...

Feel your cheeks relaxing...becoming completely loose and relaxed...feel your lips relaxing...becoming soft and relaxed...let your tongue relax...feel your nose relaxing...let your eyes relax...your eyelids are very heavy and relaxed...feel your eyebrows relaxing...and your forehead becoming smooth, cool, and relaxed...

Your whole body is now fully relaxed...

Enjoy the relaxation you are experiencing...use your left thumb and two fingers to gently squeeze your right thumb, while at the same time saying silently, "relax," anchoring the feeling of relaxation to this spot.

Experience the feeling of deep relaxation. Notice your breathing. Notice how calm and regular your breathing is...watch your breathing, without trying to change it in any way.

As you breathe in, say in your mind, "I am relaxed."

As you breathe out, mentally say, "I am calm."

I am relaxed...

I am calm...

I am relaxed...

I am calm...

Now squeeze your right thumb while mentally saying, "relax." Let the anchoring occur as this spot becomes associated with the peaceful, relaxed state you are in.

Feel the relaxation deepen each time you squeeze your right thumb while saying, "relax."

Continue to allow the relaxation to flow throughout your body... calm...peaceful...relaxed...

(Pause)

Memorize this feeling of relaxation. Notice how your body feels. Notice how calm you are. Create a picture in your mind of this state of relaxation. With this image in mind, gently squeeze your right thumb one more time while saying to yourself, "relax." Feel the relaxation deepen.

This spot is an anchor to remind you of the relaxation you are feeling right now. In the future, when you squeeze your right thumb, the feelings and memories of how relaxed you are right now will fill your mind, and your body will automatically relax.

You are as relaxed as you want to be. Calm...relaxed...

Warm...safe...comfortable...relaxed...

(Pause)

You can use anchoring any time to cue your body to relax. Remember the pleasant, peaceful state of relaxation, and know that your anchor can remind you of the relaxation you experienced.

Body 4: Affirmations

Let's begin some affirmations for self-esteem. Imagine that all the following affirmations are true for you, right now in this moment. Repeat each affirmation in your mind, or out loud, with conviction. Use your imagination to fully believe each affirmation.

The affirmations begin now.

I am at peace with myself.

I appreciate who I am.

I value myself as a person.

All people have value, and I am a valuable human being.

I deserve to relax.

I deserve to be happy.

I embrace my happy feelings, and enjoy being content.

I imagine and believe that all of these affirmations are true for me, right now in this moment.

When my mood is low, I accept my emotions and recognize that the low mood will pass, and I will be happy again. I look forward to the good times. My future is bright and positive.

I look forward to the future, and I enjoy the present.

I look fondly upon many memories from my past.

I forgive myself for my mistakes. All people make mistakes. I used to feel regret about some of my mistakes because I am a good person and want to do the best that I can, and now, I am still a good person and I release the feelings of regret because I have learned and moved on. I forgive myself for errors I have made, because I have felt bad about them long enough. I have suffered enough, and now it is time to be free. By freeing myself from past mistakes, I can move on and do good things. I forgive myself.

I feel good about who I am today.

I accept the person that I am. I accept my flaws, and accept my strengths.

I view my shortcomings as strengths not yet developed, rather than as weaknesses.

I eagerly develop new strengths.

I imagine and believe that all of these affirmations are true for me, right now in this moment.

I approach challenges with strength.

I do the best that I can at the time. I give 100% effort when I am able and when I choose to put full effort toward the things that are important. I accept my imperfections and the imperfections in what I do. My efforts are good enough, and they're okay.

I do not have to be perfect to be okay as a person.

I am a human being with flaws. I enjoy being who I am, and love myself as I am.

I nurture the child within me.

I feel secure in who I am, and do not need to compare myself to others.

All the strengths I have ever had are present in me today. I still have the same positive character, even if not all of my strengths are shown right now. I have all of those strengths of character, and will use those strengths again.

I accept myself.

I care for myself.

I take time for myself, and enjoy it. I deserve time for myself, and I feel good about taking this time regularly.

I handle difficulties with grace.

I allow myself to experience and express emotions, both negative and positive.

I accept myself.

I am perfectly alright just the way I am.

I accept myself.

I am a valuable human being.

I accept myself.

I feel confident.

I accept myself.

I feel secure.

I accept myself.

I accept myself.

Acknowledge the feelings you are experiencing after repeating the self-esteem relaxation affirmations. Accept any positive or negative feelings you are having. Allow yourself to feel calm and at peace.

Take with you the feelings of acceptance of yourself. Continue to feel positive and accepting of yourself. Hold onto this secure feeling of self-esteem as you return to your day.

Body 5: Wildlife Sanctuary

Imagine that you are walking along a path...entering a wildlife sanctuary. This sanctuary is a preserved nature area...maybe in the wilderness, or perhaps in the middle of a city.

The path is paved...just wide enough for walking. Enter the sanctuary, walking along the path. Wild grass grows beside the path, and there are trees on both sides.

Birds are singing off in the distance.

It is a beautiful, sunny day. The air is pleasant and warm, a slight breeze making it even more comfortable. Feel the sun shining down on you... warming and relaxing your body.

Take a deep breath, enjoying the fresh air. Breathe out, feeling invigorated.

Take another deep breath in...and out...

Continue to breathe the fresh, clean air.

The path curves up ahead, continuing deeper into the beautiful sanctuary.

As you continue along the path, you admire the scene around you. Small trees grow near the path, their bark smooth and light colored... small round leaves twisting gently in the breeze.

Further back from the path, larger trees grow. There is a variety of trees.

Wildflowers grow in the grass right next to the path.

As you round a curve in the path, you can see up ahead a clearing...it is a pond, or a small lake.

You can see up ahead that the path continues next to the water.

As you walk toward the water, the sun shines down, birds sing, a breeze blows...it is so peaceful here. Such a beautiful day. You feel very content.

Continue to walk toward the pond, seeing the reeds growing among the grass near the water. As you approach the pond, you can hear even more birds singing. Getting closer to the water, you see the reeds getting thicker toward the water's edge, and continuing around the shallow edges of the pool. The deeper water toward the center is smooth.

See the ducks swimming...leaving small wakes behind them...the water flowing out in a V shape as the birds slowly swim through the water.

As you continue along the path, you walk beside the pond, enjoying the sights and sounds of this sanctuary.

Up ahead, the paved trail connects with a wooden path, like a dock, that extends over the water and to a bird watching blind. This would be a wonderful place to sit.

Imagine yourself continuing along the paved trail, approaching the wooden path.

You can see more birds now, black birds with red wings darting in and out of the reeds. Geese. Loons. Sparrows. Chickadees.

A muskrat swims among the reeds, then dives under the water.

You are almost to the wooden path now. Step onto this path if you wish, walking above the reeds and the mud at the sides of the pond...now over reeds and water. The blind is located right in the middle of the reeds, but above them, so you are directly among the birds.

The blind has wooden sides, with openings that you can look through, and inside this structure there are comfortable benches where you can relax. The sides go slightly higher than the top of your head, and the top of the blind is open to the sky.

Imagine sitting on a bench, and closing your eyes for a moment to simply enjoy the sun and the peaceful sounds of the wildlife around you.

(Pause)

Look around now, at the beautiful scenery around you. The sanctuary is such a calm, serene treed area with this lake in the middle. Imagine peering through the window of the blind...look out over the water, admiring it's stillness...reflecting the blue sky and a few small white clouds. Across the water, in the distance are more trees...and beyond that, a grassy, green hill.

This scene makes a perfect picture, with water, trees, hills, and sky...

Imagine looking out another opening in the blind, looking a different direction. Look out across the reeds...along the edge of the pond. See as a deer emerges from the trees to drink from the pond, delicately stepping through the reeds to water. See the water dripping from its muzzle as the deer raises its head. The deer turns and disappears back into the trees.

Another muskrat swims by.

A colorful duck flies overhead, and spreads its wings to descend and land in the water. Water sprays and splashes out to the sides of the duck as its feet skim the surface, before finally lowering its body, folding its wings, and swimming. Another duck follows, landing in the water to swim alongside the first one.

A small bird lands right on the top edge of the blind, and looks at you, chirping pleasantly. The bird stays for a few moments before flying off.

Relax in this peaceful sanctuary. You may want to imagine laying back and closing your eyes, or continuing to look around. Imagine spending time however you wish, here in this peaceful place.

(Pause)

You are so relaxed and calm.

At peace...content.

Relax for a few moments longer in this wildlife sanctuary.

Conclusion: End of a Relaxation Script

Conclusion 1: Muscle Reawakening

Now it is time to reawaken your body and mind. When you are ready, start to move your muscles a little, feeling each muscle reawaken.

Wiggle your fingers and toes. Open your hands...then close them...and open them once again.

Roll your shoulders forward...and back...feeling your muscles reawakening.

Lean your left ear toward your left shoulder...return to the center...and move your right ear toward your right shoulder...then return to neutral.

Stretch a bit, feeling the energy flowing through your body.

Take a deep breath, reaching your arms up above your head as you inhale, and lowering your arms out to the sides and down as you exhale.

Take one more deep breath in, feeling fully alert and awake as you exhale. Return to your usual activities feeling calm and refreshed.

Conclusion 2: Breathing Awakening

Now it is time to return to your usual level of alertness and awareness. Take a deep breath in...and out.

Breathe in again...and out...

Continue to breathe smoothly and regularly, feeling your energy increasing with each breath.

As you breathe, allow your body to reawaken. Feel the energy flowing through your muscles.

Raise your shoulders as you breathe in, and lower them as you breathe out. Feel your muscles reawaken.

Keep with you the feeling of calm and relaxation, while returning to a state of wakefulness.

When you are ready, open your eyes and return to your day, feeling alert and calm.

Conclusion 3: Awareness

You are feeling calm and relaxed, and you can return to this state whenever you need to in order to feel calm and at peace.

Keep with you this feeling of relaxation while you slowly return your awareness to the present.

Keeping your eyes closed for a few moments longer, notice the surface you are on. Notice the feeling of your clothing against your skin.

Turn your attention to the sounds of your environment around you.

Feel your mind and body reawaken as your awareness of your surroundings increases.

Open your eyes, looking around you at your surroundings. Become fully aware of the environment around you.

When you have returned to your usual level of alertness, you can return to your day, feeling awake, calm, and relaxed.

Conclusion 4: Reverse Stairway

Now it is time to conclude your relaxation experience, while keeping with you a relaxed feeling.

Imagine that you are at the bottom of a stairway. At the top of the stairway is a state of alert and calm. With each step up, you become more and more awake.

Picture yourself beginning to ascend the stairway. Taking a step up, becoming slightly more awake, more alert.

Take another step up, and another, feeling your body and mind reawaken more and more with each step.

Continue up the stairway, nearing the middle of the stairway. Becoming more awake. More alert. Feeling your energy increasing, flowing through your body.

Climb further up the stairway, another stair, and another, more awake with each one. Nearing the top of the stairway. Only three steps left before you reach your usual level of awareness, feeling calm yet alert and energized.

Three...

Two...

One.

Conclusion 5: Counting Down to Sleep

You are now feeling deeply relaxed. Very deeply relaxed and calm.

You can allow this feeling of relaxation to quiet your mind even further, and drift off into peaceful sleep.

Let your mind drift...

I'll count down now from five to one. When I reach one, you will be comfortably asleep. Allow yourself to become closer and closer to deep sleep with each number...gently drift off to sleep.

Five...

Four...

Three...

Two...

One.

Conclusion 6: Counting Back

It's time now to finish your relaxation session and return to your day.

Allow your mind and body to reawaken...gradually becoming more alert. I'll count back from five. When I reach one, you will be fully awake and feeling calm and energized.

Five...becoming more awake and alert...

Four...feeling your mind and body reawaken...

Three...move your muscles a little...

Two...almost completely awake now...

One...feeling full of energy and refreshed.

Conclusion 7: Memorizing Relaxation and Counting Back

Now that you are fully relaxed, take a moment to memorize this state before returning to your usual activities.

Notice the relaxation you are experiencing. See how calm and regular your breathing is.

Take note of the relaxation in your body and the calm state of your mind.

Observe closely the feeling of relaxation, and commit the details to memory so you can remember and recreate this relaxation again whenever you need to.

Memorize this relaxed feeling.

Now that you have memorized this state of relaxation, you can reawaken your body.

I'll count up from five. Allow yourself to become more awake and alert with each number, until at one, you are completely awake and calm.

Five...

Four...

Three...

Two...

One.

Conclusion 8: Quick Stretch

Now it is time to reawaken your body and mind, and return to your day.

A quick stretch will energize you and wake up your muscles.

Open your hands...and close them...open...and close.

Reach your arms out to the sides, straight out and level at shoulder height. Hold this position. Now reach your arms forward, out to the front at shoulder height...then raise your hands up above your head. Lower your arms to your sides.

Point your toes, stretching your legs. Now raise your toes up toward the front of your legs, stretching your heels down.

Now stretch any areas that need to further awaken.

Shake your arms and shoulders gently, feeling your body completely reawaken.

Take a deep breath in...and out...and when you are ready, return to your usual activities, feeling alert and energized, yet calm.

Conclusion 9: Anchoring and Counting Back

Your whole body is now fully relaxed...

Enjoy the relaxation you are experiencing...use your left thumb and two fingers to gently squeeze your right thumb, while at the same time saying silently, "relax," anchoring the feeling of relaxation to this spot.

Experience the feeling of deep relaxation. Notice your breathing. Notice how calm and regular your breathing is...watch your breathing, without trying to change it in any way.

As you breathe in, say in your mind, "I am relaxed."

As you breathe out, mentally say, "I am calm."

I am relaxed...

I am calm...

I am relaxed...

I am calm...

Now squeeze your right thumb while mentally saying, "relax." Let the anchoring occur as this spot becomes associated with the peaceful, relaxed state you are in.

Feel the relaxation deepen each time you squeeze your right thumb while saying, "relax."

Continue to allow the relaxation to flow throughout your body... calm...peaceful...relaxed...

(Pause)

Memorize this feeling of relaxation. Notice how your body feels. Notice how calm you are. Create a picture in your mind of this state of relaxation. With this image in mind, gently squeeze your right thumb one more time while saying to yourself, "relax." Feel the relaxation deepen.

This spot is an anchor to remind you of the relaxation you are feeling right now. In the future, when you squeeze your right thumb, the feelings and memories of how relaxed you are right now will fill your mind, and your body will automatically relax.

You are as relaxed as you want to be. Calm...relaxed...

Warm...safe...comfortable...relaxed...

(Pause)

Now it is time to start to become aware of your surroundings and return to your usual level of alertness. Keep your eyes closed for a few moments while your body reawakens.

You can use anchoring any time to cue your body to relax. Remember the pleasant, peaceful state of relaxation, and know that your anchor can remind you of the relaxation you experienced.

Count back, from five to one with me, becoming more alert with each number, until at one you are fully awake and alert.

Five, becoming more awake, more alert, energetic...

Four, feeling calm, awakening even more...

Three, almost totally awake now, ready to resume with your day...

Two, eyes open, stretch the muscles, becoming completely awake...

One, fully awake, fully alert, rested and ready to go.

References

Benson, H. (1975). *The Relaxation Response*. New York: Avon Books.

www.innerhealthstudio.com

Rothschild, B. (2000). *The Body Remembers: The Psychophysiology of Trauma and Trauma Treatment*. W.W. Norton & Company, Ltd. New York, NY.

Quick Reference to Occupational Therapy, Second Edition. Kathlyn L. Reed.2001. Aspen Publishers Inc. Gaithersburg, Maryland.

Candi Raudebaugh, *Words to Relax*

About the Author

Candi Raudebaugh is an occupational therapist who specializes in mental health. She works in mental health in an acute inpatient setting and in her own private practice. Her business, Inner Health Studio, provides a website with coping skills information, relaxation scripts and audio. Her audio recordings are available every week on the *Relaxation by Inner Health Studio* Podcast.

Candi lives with her husband in Red Deer, Alberta. She enjoys reading, drawing, painting, guitar, drums, motorcycle riding, photography, travel, hiking, outdoors, computers...and, of course, website building and recording relaxation materials.

The author welcomes correspondence from readers. She may be contacted at:

Candi Raudebaugh

words-to-relax@innerhealthstudio.com
Inner Health Studio
PO Box 30036, 6380 50 Avenue
Red Deer, Alberta
Canada
T4N 1H7
www.innerhealthstudio.com

Made in the USA
Charleston, SC
18 June 2010